Business Analytics for Sales and Marketing Managers

Wiley & SAS Business Series

The Wiley & SAS Business Series presents books that help senior-level managers with their critical management decisions.

Titles in the Wiley & SAS Business Series include:

For more information on any of the above titles, please visit www.wiley.com.

Business Analytics for Sales and Marketing Managers

How to Compete in the Information Age

Gert H.N. Laursen

WILEY

John Wiley & Sons, Inc.

For general information on our other products and services or for technical
support, please contact our Customer Care Department within the United
States at (800) 762-2974, outside the United States at (317) 572-3993 or
fax (317) 572-4002.

Wiley also publishes its books in a variety of electronic formats. Some content
that appears in print may not be available in electronic books. For more
information about Wiley products, visit our web site at www.wiley.com.

ISBN 978-0-470-91286-7 (hardback); 978-1-118-03036-3 (ebk);
978-1-118-03037-0 (ebk); 978-1-118-03038-7 (ebk)

Printed in the United States of America

10 9 8 7 6 5 4 3 2 1

Contents

Preface

This book examines my favorite area: customer intelligence and analytics. I am no stranger to this field; I have been doing this for years, in the beginning passively delivering what I should, but over time growing more and more confident. In the beginning I was delivering ad hoc reports; in the end I was producing the information strategies that fueled successful company turnarounds.

At the start of my career in customer intelligence and analytics, I used phrases like these: "Information is a strategic asset," "The technical part of business intelligence is the easy part," "competing on analytics," "It is not about IT, it is about decision support." Because these terms all seemed like useful buzzwords to me, I used them. I still use these phrases today, but now I understand them. They are more than hot air—they mean something, and they are confirmed facts. I hope that by reading this book and using it actively, you will come to the same conclusion.

I was once a national training manager for an analytical company and the courses developed by my predecessor were in ANOVA, regression, neural networks, and different types of software. We had salespeople who would call customers and ask them whether they would like to buy a course in how to do regression or something else. This was a challenging assignment. If the prospective customers were already knowledgeable about the subject, they would not buy; if they did not know the topic, the salesperson could not explain what it could do for them. So we changed the way we offered the courses by providing stats for salespeople, stats for marketing people, web statistics, stats for healthcare, and so on. Suddenly prospective customers would know what they could use it for even though they still would be trained in regression, ANOVA, and neural networks.

The purpose of this book is the same. We start with what you are trying to achieve, which typically has to do with what your company or functional strategy tell you to do. Then we look into whatever means you have available. Based on this, we discuss what data to use, which analytical methods to consider, and how to implement the technical solution in a way that improves your business processes—how to create value. This book does not focus on algorithms and how they are derived; we leave that to the analysts and their software. Our focus is on business processes and how you can improve them.

If, like me, you are a pragmatic person, you should read Chapter 9, which is a case study on how to use customer analytics. This case study will show you what customer analytics can do; it is not about technology and hardware but about creativity and sound business understanding.

STRUCTURE OF THE BOOK

This book is written to be both a menu and a cookbook with a series of recipes. The menu presents the different business opportunities that can be enabled through customer analytics. You can read this menu or use it as a basis for recommendations to decision makers, who then, at a strategic or functional level, can point out which activities should be included as future projects. The menu can therefore also give you an overview of strategic opportunities that can be enabled by customer analytics.

Recipes are also included in this book. These recipes provide a more detailed description of what you should consider at an operational and project level. You can hand the relevant recipes over to the project manager or team members in charge of realizing the selected activities. In this way these people will have a first draft of the different activities that must be executed from a project perspective, including hints for the data analysts, who are the creators of decision support for customer analytics activities. Since probably no two organizations have the same business requirements, the menus included serve only as general guidelines to the final project plan. It is, however, important that you establish a clear link between the strategic situation of your organization and the opportunities offered by your information systems. These information systems provide the customer analytics options that can support and enable your organizational strategy.

The alternative to this systematic approach to selecting the right projects is a long series of interesting studies that never are going to make a change on an operational or strategic level. This is the result of too many customer analytics programs. Therefore, it is important to establish a clear link between the organizational or functional strategy and some clearly defined objectives or targets that must be met.

The following graphic illustrates the menu concept in more detail and where you can find the different elements in this book.

Themes		Chapters					
Before you start	Presenting things you need to know before you start: the concepts of this book	Introduction to the book				Chapter 1	
Strategy mapping process	Identifying focus areas based on your role, functional objective, or competitive position	Identify what you want to achieve				Chapter 2	Menu card: Strategic level
Before activities	Identifying the right activities based on your organization's maturity and how to prepare them	How to prioritize customers Chapter 3	How to get new customers Chapter 4	How to grow customers Chapter 5	How to keep customers Chapter 6		
During activities	How to maintain agility and make corrective actions during campaigns	How to monitor-success optimizing performance				Chapter 7	Menu card: Operational level and cookbook
After activities	How to make organizational learning and improve	How to take customer analytics to the next level				Chapter 8	
Example	How others have used customer analytics successfully	Case study of customer analytics				Chapter 9	

Structure of This Book

Chapter 1 provides a general introduction to the book, including a definition of customer analytics. Since customer analytics to a large extent is the same as information management within the marketing function, some of the most basic principles of information management are also presented. These basic principles will give insight into what an information system and information strategy is. We also define the terms "lead information," "lag information," and "learning information," which are used throughout this book. At the end of the chapter, we discuss segmentation and the pros and cons of basing it on data warehouse information.

In Chapter 2 you will learn how, based on your overall strategy, strategic position, functional position, or objectives, you can identify which customer relationship management (CRM) activities to focus on. Also you will be introduced to basic principles of CRM: the whale and value-based segmentation, which indicates why different customer groups should be treated differently, depending on their value to your organization. This information will allow you to reflect on your overall competitive situation and provide some overall guidance on whether you should focus on reducing customer costs, acquiring new customers, cross- and up-selling activities, or retaining your existing customer base. Typically a company should be involved with all these commercial activities. However, you might find that your strategic focus needs some recalibration.

Chapter 3 describes how to make and implement a value-based segmentation, which is a shared organizational view on which customer to focus on. This chapter discusses the basic concepts of project and change management, since a value-based segmentation will affect all functions and processes in an organization. Later chapters refer to some of these principles.

Chapter 4 explains how customer analytics improve your customer acquisition processes through the use of data warehouse data, questionnaire data, and interviews with subject matter experts individually and in combination. This chapter also presents another essential marketing and process improvement concept: needs-based segmentation.

Chapter 5 presents various ways you can improve your sales processes to existing customers, which ranges from replacement sales, and increased share of wallet, to cross-selling efforts. As in Chapters 4 and 6, we take into account different information and organizational maturity levels. This chapter also shows you how to make a shared data foundation for sales processes to existing customers and to increase the customer lifetime as presented in Chapter 6.

Chapter 6 presents various ways of increasing the customer lifetime, known as churn prediction, customer retention, or win-back. The methods of customer retention will vary depending on whether you take a marketing, customer service, or process excellence perspective.

Chapter 7 describes how to create and use lag information. The focus of Chapters 3 through 6 was on how to create information that will enable significant process improvements, also known as lead information. Lag information is used for monitoring and controlling existing processes. (You might already know this concept as performance management.) This chapter also contains a more detailed discussion than the one in Chapter 1 about the difference between lead and lag information.

Chapter 8 takes a deeper look at the third information concept presented in this book—learning information—which has to do with knowledge management, that is, how to make organization-wide use of the insights gained in your customer analytics or marketing department. These insights can be fed to other commercial units and used as a feedback to the strategic planning function. Knowledge sharing to other commercial organizational units typically deals with knowledge management systems. Feedback to the strategy planning unit moreover involves aligning the customer analytics processes with the strategic expectations; therefore, the chapter presents more information on process maturity, which serves as a benchmark for whether your customer analytics are up to the required level and presents ways to identify which elements seem to be lagging.

Chapter 9 provides a case study of how a company turnaround driven by customer analytics got a leading Danish telecom provider back in the black. This case study is included to give you a practical feel for how customer analytics can be used. Read this chapter if you feel that you do not have a clear understanding of what customer analytics is.

Acknowledgments

I would like to express my gratitude to my wife and children—Mahak, Victoria, and Lucas—and my in-laws—Maryam and Muhammad—who stepped in and took over my responsibilities, allowing me to sit in the Royal Library of Copenhagen while writing this book.

CHAPTER 1

Introduction

T his first chapter provides guidance about the opportunities of customer analytics, given the strategic objectives and the maturity of the information systems in your organization. It also introduces the basic terms used in the rest of this book, including the term "customer analytics," and how it deviates from terms such as "business intelligence" (BI) and "customer intelligence." Like business intelligence and business analytics (BA), however, customer analytics is part of the same discipline called information management, a term that also is investigated further.

This chapter also discusses different types of information, which are grouped from a process perspective. There is also a section introducing process management. Finally, the chapter discusses what segmentation is, including the strengths and weaknesses of segmentation based on input from data warehouse (DW), questionnaire, and subject matter experts.

DEFINITION OF CENTRAL CONCEPTS USED IN THIS BOOK

In my previous book, *Business Analytics for Managers: Taking Business Intelligence beyond Reporting*,[1] I defined "business analytics" as:

> Delivering the right decision support to the right people
> at the right time.

This definition points out some key points to those working with BI (decision support based on simple reports) or BA (decision support based on complex analytical skills) for the first time:

- The purpose of all the data, technical expressions, servers, architectural strategies, master data management, and so on is to create decision support—that is all. The value from a DW is enabled via increased organization-wide ability to make better decisions.

- The creation of decision support based on electronically stored data involves various technical departments, analysts, and end users spread around the organization. Some clear processes must be in place for the organization to reap the full benefits of its BI investment.

Business intelligence has the potential to provide decision support to all of the functions in an organization. Using BI, the human resources department can learn which individuals in an organization are high performers and then hire, train, and reward other employees to become similar high performers. BI enables inventory managers to minimize the amount of capital in stored goods while being able to deliver what is needed. Production can minimize its costs by setting up activity-based costing programs, and so on.

The purpose for all the functions mentioned is: to optimize performance within the area for which they are responsible. The same is the case with customer analytics; it is decision support with the overall purpose of optimizing the lifetime of your customer base. Hence we define customer analytics as:

> Delivering customer-centric decision support to the right
> people at the right time.

Typically, three types of decision makers in an organization are involved in customer analytics, developing a company strategy, a marketing strategy, and an operational-level strategy:

1. **Strategic decision makers.** These are the individuals who make the overall company strategy. To do so, they need

customer-centric information to make the best possible plan for how to run the company in the future. They also need information about whether the overall strategy is being executed successfully or whether corrective action needs to be taken.

2. **Sales and marketing decision makers.** These are the individuals who make the sales and the customer relationship management (CRM) strategy. The sales strategy deals with getting new customers, and the CRM strategy deals with handling the existing customer base. Just like the strategic decision makers, they need information to create business activities and to monitor their execution. The difference is the level of details: The sales and marketing department wants the information on a short-term, campaign/market activity level; the strategy team typically requires information on an overall level, to spot trends and long-term business opportunities.

3. **Operation decision makers.** These are the people who implement the campaigns and market activities, typically in sales and call centers. The decision support they require is in terms of whom to call, when and what to offer, or what to say in order to retain dissatisfied customers. These decision makers are the users of operational information, which could include call lists and pop-ups when customers call in, along with performance management reports.

There is, however, one very important distinction between the BA/BI and customer analytics/customer intelligence that has to do with the process value chain. The BI/BA process is fed, more or less exclusively, by DW data. My earlier book on BA showed the various kinds of decision support that is enabled via a DW and how this process should be managed. This book has less to do with where the data are coming from and more to do with how you can make the right customer-centric decisions. Therefore, the focus is not on whether the data are sourced from a DW, questionnaire data, or the insights gained from subject matter experts, as long as the decision support is customer-centric and some analytics are used in the process. The various data and knowledge sources should not be seen as competing sources but rather as supplementary elements that generate significant synergies.

As you learn in this book, the synergies vary, depending on the maturity of your processes, the degree of existing customer understanding in your organization, and the quality of the various data sources.

MORE THAN JUST TECHNICAL SOLUTIONS

As mentioned earlier, if you only see customer analytics and BI as technical solutions, you will fail, since they are about helping people make better decisions. Once I was part of an implementation of a customer scorecard (a tool that lists what the company had delivered to customers, including whether it was meeting service-level agreements). We learned that even though it is obvious that the sales staff should use such a tool in order to conduct fact-based negotiations with their counterparts, only one-third of them used it. Some did not know about this new tool; others preferred to do it the old way, even though the new method provided a wide-range of process improvements to customers. Of the one-third who used the scorecard, we estimated that they got only one-third of the potential value out of it because they did not apply that information in an optimal way. In other words, if you see customer analytics or any other information system as only a technical discipline, you will realize only a fraction of its potential value—just the tip of the iceberg.

The obvious shortcoming was that the makers of the scorecard had implemented only a technical solution, since they did not consider business processes and the users. The change management element was missing.

We mentioned earlier that there are three types of decision makers. Since the one-third of the one-third rule does not apply to them all, we will go through them one by one.

■ **Strategic decision makers.** As mentioned earlier, they basically do two things: They make strategies and follow up on them. When you make strategy, you focus on two things: levering short-term issues and seeking to gain long-term competitive advantages. Research has shown that most organizations do not understand the full potential of information, including customer analytics, during the strategy-making process. One reason for this could be that most chief information officers do not have an analytical and strategic background.

■ **Sales and marketing decision makers.** If the person responsible for making the sales and CRM strategy is not aware of the potential of customer analytics, how can they be expected to opt for it? This is also why we have made this book a menu that shows the relationship between some universal key performance indicators and individual methodologies. At the same time, the analyst has to be able to deliver. That is what we call the recipe, which contains input about what information and knowledge should be delivered before a new business activity is started and how to monitor it.

■ **Operation decision makers.** As mentioned, you cannot just make some pop-up window in a call center and expect to realize the full effect of whatever intentions were behind it. If you want the full effect of an information system, you must go through three steps during the implementation phase:

1. **Make process maps that clearly define how you wish people to work.** For example, when a customer calls in, what do you want staff to say in order to clarify the customer requirements? If you do not already have a clear idea about how to identify what the customer wants, then go out and find some best practices. The use of best practices also means that you already have identified a process improvement at this early step.

2. **Design a technical system that supports this best practice.** For example, when people call in, a pop-up with relevant customer details is shown, so that the agent does not have to ask the customer about what you as a company already know. If the customer issue is resolved positively, a pop-up informing the call center agent about potential cross-selling opportunities could occur. A bonus system rewarding call center agents for their selling efforts (and ability to solve issues) also could be established.

3. **Train the call center agents to follow the new procedures that you wish to implement, including the**

technical solution and the bonus system. The process and training elements are also known as change management elements; they are ways to lead people into following new ways of working and keeping them doing so after you have left the building.

WHAT IS AN INFORMATION STRATEGY?

In this section we take a closer look at what an information strategy is in order to make the link between the company strategy and what decision support has to be produced. We also introduce different kinds of information, based on which kind of decision support this information is made to support. Finally, this section also gives insights on why so many customer analytics projects that are driven by the DW fail. Since customer analytics often sources its data from one or more DWs, this section is explicitly from a BI perspective. As you will learn, BI based on DW data is a very complex process, and there are important lessons to be learned.

First of all, we take a closer look at what an information strategy is. In the simplest form, an information strategy can be described as a list of all the knowledge and information that is required in order for a business strategy to be successful, including a plan of how to create this decision support or operational data. Adding a little complexity to this definition, an information strategy consists of three domains that have to be managed and aligned in order to use DW information successfully:

1. **Business requirements.** Without clear business requirements on the overall objectives of your company strategy or marketing plan, over time your business activities will end up as a patchwork based on what you used to do with no clear strategic direction. After all, there is no point in making a plan that has no purpose, so the first requirement is clear objectives.

2. **Analytical competencies.** Without knowing which analytical competencies are available and needed at certain times, you will end up continuously reusing the same analytical skills you have always used, which is the same as degenerating your

decision support. As they say, if you have a hammer in the hand, everything looks like a nail. Therefore, you need a full analytical tool box and the knowledge of how to use it. This is business critical in the information age where "survival of the smartest" is the winning and constantly changing formula.

3. **Data foundation.** Customer analytics, like all other types of BI, is based on making the most out of data stored in different data repositories. If for various reasons you cannot get access to data or understand, trust, and manipulate the data you are receiving, your analytical efforts all stop here. In other words, you should work together with the DW team and the technical side of the organization, but in case of conflicts, you have to make it clear to them that the technical side of the organization is there to support the commercial. It can never be the other way around.

If this is all there is to it, then why do 50% to 70% of all customer analytics projects fail or end up being challenged because they do not deliver the expected returns? Why is it that if you start a new customer analytics activity with an average customer analytics team, you should expect to fail? Many reasons for this primarily have to do with the fact that these are cross-functional activities that require top specialist skills from everyone in the process. Therefore, even if only one individual, step, or function in the process fails, the whole process will fail. In my previous book, *Business Analytics for Managers* (www.basm-support.com), I explained this process in great detail. In this section, I just present the overall model, the information wheel (see Exhibit 1.1).

The information wheel shows that information management starts with a business strategy: Strategy is king. Based on the overall business strategy, each of the functions (human resources, sales, finance, etc.) will make its own functional strategies in alignment with each other to deliver the functional specific objectives (e.g., to reduce employee turnover to 5% per year, increase sales by 20%, or minimize outstanding to 14 days in average). Because this book is about customer analytics, we focus only on the sales and marketing strategies. In general, their objectives can be described as optimizing customer

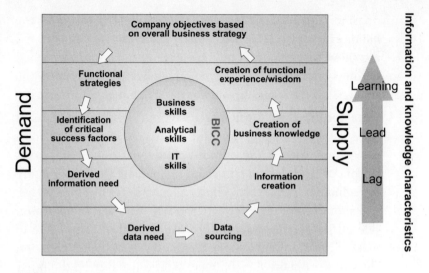

Exhibit 1.1 Information Wheel from an Organizational Perspective

acquisitions processes, cross-selling and up-selling processes, and retention processes. In other words, their aim is to get, to increase, and to keep customers.

Sales and marketing processes are very often referred to as CRM processes because, overall, this is what they are about: managing how we treat our customers. In many organizations, the sales process is separated out into a sales department for various reasons. From a process perspective, however, the sales and the CRM department are closely linked. This is because if the sales department acquires disloyal and low-spending customers, the CRM department will be set up for failure, with its members spending their time trying to cultivate customers with a low preference for the company, brand, service, or product, or low spending.

For both the sales and the CRM strategy or all major activities, strategy creators identify the critical success factors (usually about four to six factors). All of these factors must go correctly in order for the strategy to be successful as a whole. For example, imagine a marketing department strategic objective that states that the customer base should be increased by 5% at the end of the year. The marketing department now has the option of acquiring more customers or retaining more customers. Either way or a combination of the two ways will meet the objective.

If the CRM department chooses to embark on a pure retention strategy, to be successful, it is critical that it launches the right activities, toward the right customers, with the right retention offers, at the right time. Also, the CRM department will require some performance statistics to evaluate the campaigns continuously and to what degree they are meeting their overall strategic objectives.

We have now defined the critical success factors, which in turn define the derived information need, which can be formulated to analysts in this way: Tell us which customers will leave us, when, and why. Then the business must figure out what to do about it (i.e., develop the retention offers). The business also would like to get data that indicates how well the activities perform on a running basis.

Based on the derived information need, business analysts will start searching for data that can provide input to their data-mining models and statistical efforts. Perhaps the data already exist; alternatively, they will have to be sourced in the future or perhaps the company will have to continue without it.

When this is done, the analysts create the data. This needed information can be:

- **Lead information.** Information used for innovating new processes (before your new campaigns).

- **Lag information.** Performance data used for monitoring the performance of the existing processes (used during the campaign execution phase).

- **Learning information.** Feedback to the strategy function and other parallel sales departments allowing them to see new opportunities and threats based on the overall learning from the historical marketing activities (created after a campaign).

As can be seen, creation of the needed information and knowledge is a complex process where there is no room for mistakes. Most business analysts are specialists (although sometimes they may lack skills or simply be generalists in disguise), and typically no process owner is in place. In some organizations, BI competence centers formalize some of the contacts; however, most organizations rely on the generalist skills of project managers to make all ends meet.

In addition, the change management program of training the call centers must be undertaken. Agents must be trained in outbound calls or receiving campaign replies, and internal procedures must be in place. Potentially, technical solutions may have to be in place before kickoff, and external partners may have to perform in alignment.

Due to their complexity, it is no wonder that customer analytics activities typically fail. In fact, one might wonder why things occasionally go well. It is important to understand that customer analytics activities that are partly or fully based on DW data are a complex endeavor since they require specialist skills and you will rely on many other functions in the organization. For these reasons your analysts should have business, analytical, and data skills, plus people and project skills. A limited number of these people are available, and they are hard to keep, but if you do: They are worth their salaries.

REVOLUTIONARY VERSUS EVOLUTIONARY PROCESS CHANGES

This section adds a process perspective on how to make customer analytics, in order to explain the different kinds of information, such as lead, lag, and learning information. In this context, we define a process as a series of coordinated actions with a common goal in mind. The goal could be to sell a pair of shoes to a customer, and the process could be to pull a list of customers who have not purchased any shoes from our Web site lately, identify which kinds of shoes that each would be most likely to buy, and then send the offer to the customer by email.

If you are the process owner, there are two ways you can improve this process: through evolutionary or revolutionary changes. The corresponding information types and the way that you typically work with them can be divided into two categories: lead and lag information. The two ways of optimizing a process are:

1. **Evolutionary business process changes have to do with optimizing already existing processes within their existing framework.** Typically these changes are triggered by the

people who operate them based on such information as control charts and reports, which document the historical performance of the process in play, or simply by clever and engaged employees.

2. **Revolutionary business changes have to do with reconfiguring a process by abandoning existing ones or developing new ones where needed.** Typically these changes are triggered by the functional strategy team because the existing processes are no longer up to market standards or because the organizational strategy has changed, which of course is reflected in how things are done: the processes. The information required for revolutionary business changes typically is derived via the use of analytical procedures and techniques.

In other words, a process performs in an acceptable way according to market standards and business ambition. Hence we will monitor it via reports and the like. Alternatively, we find that the process (e.g., the way we sell or what we sell) does not live up to market standards, and we need to generate knowledge about what customers want and need. This information can come from many places, such as subject matter experts, questionnaires, or DW data. This process perspective is outlined in Exhibit 1.2, where the flat line depicts ever-increasing market standards that continuously require the organization to

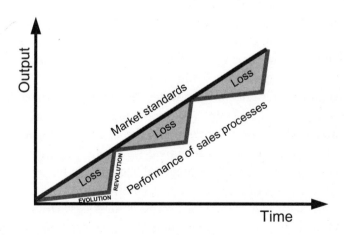

Exhibit 1.2 Stairway Model Illustrating One Process

produce at lower costs and create offers that give higher user satisfaction.

The lower zigzag line represents the nature of a typical business process or product that has to satisfy ever-increasing market demands. The zigzag shape is a result of the nature of processes. When processes are implemented, they typically do live up to the market requirements; however, they do not improve with the speed of the market. Typically the same product will come in new versions, which would be evolutionary change, but at some point in time the product simply does not live up to market standards and new product lines must replace the old ones. The way we optimally price things changes over time, the optimal customer service changes, the optimal way of branding changes; the same is true with our commercials, the way we get customers, and the way we keep our customers: The requirements all change over time. Sometimes evolutionary versions will do, but sometimes nothing less than new innovative products and services are needed.

For example, try to imagine a society where there is no innovation because all of the inhabitants do not like risk taking, innovation, or new ideas, or simply are so focused on getting their daily bread that they do not have time to think beyond what they do today. What you would get is a society where everyone would ride in horse carts instead of automobiles; however, no doubt, they would use the horses in the most efficient manner. The problem is that all you have done is change an inefficient process and turn it into to an optimized inefficient process. You also often see this in high-performance organizations with mediocre management. People have to run faster and faster in order to keep up with the competition simply because they did not work smarter—they do not innovate. This method will work for a while, but only for a while. This model also illustrates this via the "loss" areas, which show the consequences of the specific process not being up to date. The loss is generated via an inefficient process that is too costly or missed market potential because the process does not satisfy the customer needs in one way or another.

All the sales and marketing processes for a company also could be illustrated by a line rather than steps, where the line shows the average distance of all the marketing processes from the market

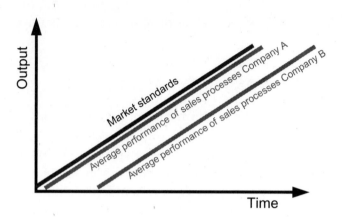

Exhibit 1.3 Stairway Model Illustrating the Averages of Many Processes

standard. The farther the line is away from the market standards, the less competitive the company will be. Such a scenario is illustrated in Exhibit 1.3, which shows a situation in which company A is more competitive than company B.

From this graph, we can conclude that, in order to remain competitive, a company has to configure its process landscape (in this example sales and marketing processes) according to market needs. The big question is how to do this. From an information management perspective, the answer is by continuously generating lead information that can revolutionize your processes when needed and by continuously generating lag information that allows you to monitor and optimize your existing processes between the revolutionary changes. You also have to keep in mind that innovation does not stop at the point where the product meets market standards. Innovation can set new market standards. If these new market standards are a result of your analytical processes, among others, then you are competing on analytics.

Therefore, the ultimate purpose of customer analytics is to give your business agility—the ability to react fast to market changes. It is all about agility, being able to make the right decisions at the right time (e.g., when to launch new campaigns and what they should be about, when to develop new products and in what direction, when to improve the way you do deliver your service and what is good enough, when to react on competitive moves and what to do about it, etc.).

SEGMENTATION AND DATA WAREHOUSING

This section discusses what segmentation is as well as how to implement a segmentation model. The way you can use a segmentation model is closely linked to whether it is also present in a DW or another organization-wide data repository or whether this segmentation is an abstract idea existing only on a PowerPoint level.

The basic idea behind segmentation is that customers have different needs, wants, values, behaviors, and so on. In an ideal world, we would of course like to treat every customer individually and according to his or her specific needs and values. Practically, however, very often this will not work because we simply do not have information about the individual customers' needs and wants, and acquiring this information would be too costly, if the customer was willing to give it to us in the first place. In cases where we have this information on a customer level, customers might not be willing to pay us what it costs to deliver and produce tailor-made goods according to their individual requirements. There are, of course, many examples of customer-made production that is successful. However, there are also many where it is not—just think about the whole historical shift from carpenters to mass-produced IKEA furniture. Therefore, the optimal number of segments is a matter of balancing between the costs of individualization versus to what extent customers are willing to pay for this customization.

In this book, we categorize customers in many ways: whom you should sell more to and who is valuable to us according to different customer needs, and so on. One central lesson here is that you should stop thinking about segmentation as if there is only one dimension to see customers through and start talking about needs-based segmentation, value-based segmentation, segments ready for different kinds of up-selling, cross-selling based segmentation, communication-based segmentation, churn-based segmentation, segmentation based on dunning procedures, risk-based segmentation, and more. This might sound confusing, but you also learn that customers vary in many ways, and each way can form a basis for segmentation. After all, segmentation is just grouping customers as a result of some sort of similarity.

SEGMENTATION BASED ON DATA WAREHOUSE INFORMATION

Throughout this book, there is an ongoing discussion about two ways of doing needs-based segmentation depending on whether it is generated from a DW or from questionnaire data, where needs-based segmentation is defined as a categorization of customers with similar buying criteria, which could be based on prize or different product features like the safety of a car, the comfort of a car, the carbon footprint of a car.

If your needs-based segmentation is based on DW data, to a certain extent, the segmentation must have been created based on your own organization's customer information through the use of analytic techniques. The benefit of this sort of analysis is that it is relatively easy to make segmentations of your full customer base (depending on your data quality). That is, you know on a one-to-one basis which customers belong to which segment. This is in contrast to a situation where you have five segments based on an abstract segmentation model, but you do not know which customers fall into which of the five categories.

Internet-based companies are an interesting example of stores that naturally could focus on a one-to-one relationship with their customers since they have vast amounts of transactional data from the web logs and eventual transactions. These web logs can inform companies about how the customers came to their homepage, how they click around, who purchases what and how often, what typically is purchased together, and the home addresses of those who made physical purchases. Pop-up surveys are easy to include in this media. Other types of organizations that typically have very detailed customer information are banks, telecom operators, and insurance companies, since their services typically are subscription based, they know their customers on a one-to-one basis, and the interactions can be electronically stored and used for later analysis.

SEGMENTATION BASED ON NON–DATA WAREHOUSE INFORMATION

If you have no customer base or available data about it or if the DW data simply do not give you some actionable segments, you can be forced to go for non–DW segmentation. You can segment your customers based on many sources as well as combined sources. Typically, however, your segmentation logic will be based on input from subject matter experts or simply will be dictated by your organization or external business partners. If your segmentation logic is based on questionnaires, the types of segmentation can be the same as with DW-based segmentations, such as needs-based or value-based segmentation; however, often this methodology allows you to segment only those customers in your customer base who replied to your questionnaire, since for obvious reasons you do not know anything about the needs of the nonrespondents. The benefit of segmentation based on non–DW data is that you can base it on a wider set of information, since in questionnaires you can ask about whatever you want, as opposed to segmentations based on the DW, where the customer attributes that your segmentation is based on is limited to the data currently stored by your organization.

Often larger companies with subscription-based funding need both DW– and non–DW–based segmentation, since they wish to run campaigns through the mass media and at the same time have CRM activities below the media line, such as emails and direct mail. Often there is no alignment between the media-relevant and the CRM-relevant segmentation models. One way of aligning these two is to make a series of customers, categorize which segment they belong to via a questionnaire, then identify the characteristics of the same customers based on DW data, and finally categorize the rest of the customers in the DW according to these characteristics.

As mentioned earlier, there are many ways to develop a segmentation model. The best one is probably defined by looking at what you want to achieve, the costs and the benefits of the different approaches, the usefulness of your DW, and the long-term strategic objectives and key stakeholders. There are, however, some elementary points that can serve as a strong indicator of which direction you should pursue.

First of all, the DW–based segmentation model is very powerful for companies that are focused on CRM activities executed via below the media line through email activities, personal calls, and written mail. Such companies know their customers on a one-to-one level. Alternatively, externally based segmentation (based on subject matter experts or questionnaires) is a very natural tool for companies that do not know their customers by name or are focused on acquisition through mass media activities. Examples of such companies are traditional stores where there is no registration of who purchased what or how many times a customer visited a store.

Regardless of how you get to your DW–based segmentation, there needs to be an alignment between your acquisition processes and the way you treat your existing customer base. From a customer experience perspective, there should be a sense of continuity from what you expect to get when you become a customer to what you get when you have become a customer. From an organizational perspective, confusion and lack of engagement from the rest of the organization can result if the market intelligence department promotes one version of the truth used for acquisition activities, while the customer analytics department promotes another customer view for CRM purposes. In such cases, the rest of the organization will not know what it should deliver in order satisfy the customers.

OTHER CONSIDERATIONS

In general, a segmentation model, like most other tools, is only as good as those who use it. Therefore, if you are responsible for developing a segmentation model, the first thing you should consider is who could potentially use it. The exercise is relatively simple. First, sit down with an organization map and identify all the different functional areas and processes. For each of these potential users, brainstorm how customer segmentation could add value to each individual functional area or process. After you finish this homework, start setting up meetings with existing and potential stakeholders, and agree on what they really want. One stakeholder that should be of particular interest is the strategic department; if it adapts your way of doing segmentation, your organization will become increasingly customer centric in its future method of going to market. The strength of a top-down implementation is that since a company strategy is signed off by top management, you will automatically get their buy-in. Thus, you have taken a first step into treating your customers consistently across all channels (which is an absolute basic in marketing). If your segmentation is based on DW information, you will also be able to report monthly on each segment in terms of how many new customers you get, turnover, complaints, how many leave you; this is essential feedback to the strategy department. The saying "You can't manage what you can't measure" therefore becomes very relevant here, since a strategy department will only develop a strategy plan based on organization objectives that can be factually measured.

NOTE

1. Gert Laursen and Jesper Thorlund, *Business Analytics for Managers: Taking Business Intelligence beyond Reporting* (Hoboken, NJ: John Wiley & Sons, 2010).

CHAPTER 2

Identify What You Want to Achieve: The Menu on a Strategic Level

What if I told you which overall customer activities you should pursue as a direct result of your current competitive situation—would that be of interest?

The purpose of this chapter is to enable you to make a link from your competitive situation to a selection of some specific customer activities. Using the menu metaphor, this means understanding the overall needs of the individuals at the table, which could range from breakfast or a nine-course dinner to a need for quick dish for a person allergic to peanuts. This chapter does not provide guidance about which specific course to serve but greatly narrows down the alternatives (e.g., something light with fish). Armed with this knowledge, you will know where on the menu to find the desired dish including its recipe. This chapter also provides guidance about which of the chapters in this book you should focus on.

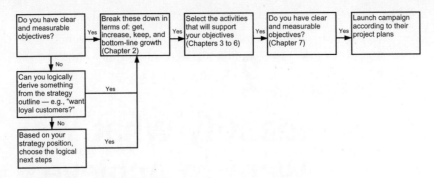

Exhibit 2.1 Activity Mapping Process

Exhibit 2.1 suggests in more detail how you can identify which customer-analytic activities to pursue, based on how this book has been structured. First, you should identify your objectives or whether some specific activities already are an expected delivery from your department. If not, from reading this chapter, you will get a clear idea about which activities you can promote to your stakeholders. Chapters 3 through 6 will help you identify how to develop and implement these activities, based on the maturity of your organization. Once stakeholders have signed off on some specific activities, you will be able to use Chapters 3 through 6 as input for your project plans, since these chapters suggest the data and analytical requirements and explain how your project plan could look.

In this chapter we describe two central concepts: the whale and value-based segmentation. These two concepts combined can also suggest a generic customer relationship management (CRM) strategy if you have no clear guidance from your stakeholders or from your company strategy. Finally, at the end of the chapter you can find an analytical approach on how to identify relevant CRM activities.

It is important that you see the top-down approach (based on your competitive situation) and the bottom-up approach (based on data) not as competing but as mutually supportive.

PRESENTING THE WHALE

The name of the whale model comes from its shape, which resembles a whale with its tail under the water and its body above. In the model the horizontal line does not depict a waterline but a timeline going from the first contact with a customer until the customer-vendor relation ultimately ends. In the middle there is a line that points out the time of the first sale—the point in time from where the sales efforts start to pay. (See Exhibit 2.2.)

The height of the whale's profile depicts the earnings of the customer. In the beginning there were no earnings, just acquisition costs; however, because we manage to convert this relationship all the way from a prospect to a customer, this whale has a body depicted above the timeline. We could imagine that there would be a whole lot of tails with no bodies illustrating all the sales attempts that had not been successful, yet that would be wrong since the tail describes the cost of the campaign divided by the number of acquisition. This way we will see that if one campaign generates only one customer, the area of the tail would describe the full campaign costs. Thus, as a rule, good campaigns would have small tails relative to their bodies.

The body of the whale illustrates the customer's earnings and can be estimated as the average earnings per month multiplied by the number of months you had the customer. We can now define the customer lifetime value as the earnings of a customer minus the acquisition costs, as shown in the next equation.

Acquisition costs per customer –
(Average earnings for customer per time × Lifetime)

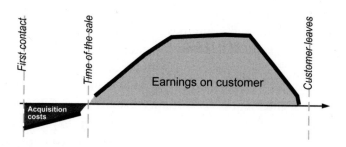

Exhibit 2.2 The Whale

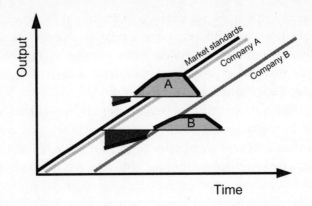

Exhibit 2.3 Whales on Stairways

From this simple formula we now know that there are at least three ways in which customer analytics can enable the profitability of your customer base:

1. Reducing your acquisition costs (see Chapter 4)
2. Selling more per time unit to the customers (see Chapter 5)
3. Retaining the customers for longer time (see Chapter 6)

Exhibit 2.3 shows the relationship between the stairway model (presented in Chapter 1) and the whale. In the example, Company A's sales and marketing process are close to the best standards in the market. Company B, however, is not up to the same market standards. In this example, Company B suffers on two of the three dimensions: relatively high acquisition costs and relatively low customer earnings per month.

From this example it seems as if Company B has some costly or poor sales processes, and it also has to look into how it handles additional sales to existing customers. Potentially the company also could be attracting low-end customers who never are going to give it a high monthly turnover. This leads us on to the second essential concept: value-based segmentation or customer value estimation. You must recognize that not all customers are equally profitable to you. Therefore, the big question is: Which customers are valuable to you? Even more important: How can you improve or control their value?

CUSTOMER VALUE ESTIMATION

The basic idea behind customer value estimation is that not all customers are equally valuable; there are customers who are very valuable and customers whom you lose money on serving. You can rarely blame the customers for being unprofitable; after all, we set the price and define what the services or products are. Nevertheless, in a world where costs constantly have to be reduced, you will have situations where customers are queuing (as with a call center, to get into a restaurant, for the best seats, etc.), which will create some customer dissatisfaction and lead to question: Which customers would you prefer not to risk losing? The logical answer is that if a low-value customer calls and then a high-value customer calls, the high-value customer should always get through first. If you lose the low-value customer, it is of less cost to you because your way of doing business is simply not configured to this type of customer. This all links back to the company strategy, or the way by which you have decided to do business. Your strategy is based on some choice of which customer segments to pursue.

If you have unprofitable customers in your customer base, you could consider raising prices to them in order to make them profitable. If they leave, so be it; they do not fit into your business model in the first place, and now you lose less money.

Presenting the Model

Exhibit 2.4 presents the basic idea of dividing customers into categories according to their value. You might already have heard about the 80-20 rule, which states that you make 80% of your turnover or earnings on the top 20% of your customers. The 80-20 rule is marked with a circle in the graph showing that to the left of it, on the horizontal axis, you will find the 20% most profitable customers. Below the circle, on the vertical axis, you will find the 80% of the total turnover.

For this example's segmentation purpose, we will not use the 20% mark but simply divide the customers into three equally large groups and call them gold, silver, and bronze customers. The graph then tells

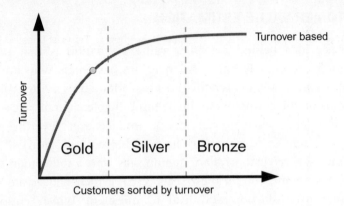

Exhibit 2.4 Turnover-Based Segmentation

us that the gold segment generates by far most of our turnover; the silver segment generates a little; and the bronze segment generates hardly any additional turnover. In this example, the curve is very bent. If all of our customers paid a fixed subscription for a flat-rate product, the line would shift toward a flat diagonal line going from the bottom left and up to the top right corner.

Obviously it makes more sense to make a value-based segmentation based on what we earn on our customers. Practically that means that we should include the variable costs that we can assign directly to a customer. For the telecommunications industry, this could include:

- **Interconnect cost.** The amount we need to pay to another network/telecom provider because the customer uses its network.
- **Customer service costs.** Inbound calls by customers to the call center that are not caused by the telecom operator.
- **Uncovered dunning costs.**
- **Costs of letters.** Costs if the customer could have information sent to an email address; and so on.

There could also be additional earnings for customers:

- **Interconnect earnings.** What we earn from other persons calling our customer from other networks, which subsequently can be charged to other network providers.

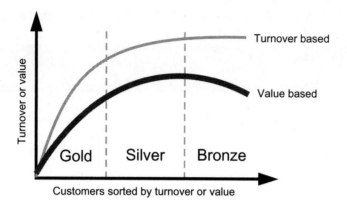

Exhibit 2.5 Value-Based Segmentation

- **What the customer buys in our shops.**
- **Potential earnings from the dunning process.**

It would also be logical to make the segmentation on a customer level rather than a phone number/subscription level, since the decision makers whose behavior we are about to change could be a company or family, where only one key decision maker pays for all the subscriptions.

After making these changes, we can make a new line called a value-based segmentation (see Exhibit 2.5). Some interesting observations about this line are listed next.

- The line is placed lower than on the turnover-based segmentation since, in this example, there are fewer additional earnings than variable costs in the model.
- The 80-20 rule still seems to be intact.
- For the bronze segment, the slope is negative, which means that we lose money on each of these customers (they do not help us in covering our fixed costs).
- The turnover-based line is on a subscription level and represents a larger number of observations than the black line, which is on a customer level, since customers can have many subscriptions and not the other way around.

Exhibit 2.6 Telecommunication Industry Example on How Costs Can Move Customers and Subscriptions

	Turnover-based segmentation (before)		
	Gold	Silver	Bronze
Value-based segmentation (black line) Gold	15%	6%	5%
Silver	8%	21%	8%
Bronze	4%	10%	23%

Exhibit 2.6, an example from the telecommunication industry, shows that more than 40% of the customers changed value segments depending on whether we included the costs of serving the customer when making a value-based segmentation model. In other words, customers with high turnover often are not the profitable ones; thus, it is important to include costs in your value-based segmentation model.

Adding Business Rules

Often it is important to add some business rules on top of your value-based segmentation model in order for it to take into account more factors. Some examples are presented next.

- New customers are classified as silver customers for the first three months unless they spend like gold customers, which will upgrade them. We might do this if value-based segmentation is based on the average spending over the last three months. Customers are extremely sensitive in the early phases of a new business relationship, which is why we want to make sure that new ones are treated well during the early phases.

- If we reward a customer with a handset, this cost should not affect the value-based segmentation. (We want to avoid a situation where we reward gold customers by turning them into silver customers.)

- If the dunning department tells us that there is a high risk that a customer will not pay his or her debts, we should downgrade the customer into a lower segment to reflect that risk. We cannot give new handsets to customers who do not pay their bills. If this risk probability is derived from historical behavior, we can inform the customer about these consequences and upgrade him or her for using direct debit or prepayment.

■ If you actively use your value-based segmentation in direct customer communication, consider using turnover-based segmentation with tougher selection criteria, since value-based segmentation can be very hard to explain to customers who have high bills generated via, for example, international calls, where the foreign network owner makes all the profits and the customer is less valuable to your network.

■ When applying value-based segmentation to your business customers, often it is beneficial to make value-based segmentation on two different measurements. Customers who have many subscriptions are scored on an index variable of 0 to 200 with a mean of 100, so that customers with an average number of subscriptions get the score 100; if they score less than average, they get an index number somewhere between 0 and 99. The second measurement is the average consumption per subscription, again scored on an index variable from 0 to 200. Base your value-based segmentation on an average of these two scores. Small customers (in terms of number of subscriptions) with high earnings per subscription will enjoy the same level of benefits as large customers (in terms of subscriptions) with little value per subscription.

As business rules and cost drivers change frequently over time, it is recommended that the segmentation be owned by the CRM or marketing department and generated in analytical and data management tools like SAS or SPSS as a monthly list to the data warehouse. Alternatively, you will end up in a situation where your response should be counted in months rather than in hours when changes have to be made—that is, if the information technology department has time and can do it in the first place. It will take experienced data analysts a month or two to set up a value-based segmentation, including automating it via open database connectivity (ODBC) connections in a SAS or SPSS tool on a $1,000 personal computer in complex cases, such as the telecommunication industry, for solutions covering 10 million customers. Because you will need to buy the software and hire the analyst anyway if you want to compete on customer analytics, the start-up costs actually can be considered overhead costs.

FROM STRATEGY TO MENU

So far we have presented two models in this chapter. These two models are essential concepts of this book since they can help you to break down your objectives into the four core value disciplines within sales and CRM and help you make a generic CRM strategy.

As shown in Exhibit 2.7, the four value disciplines that also will be presented individually through Chapters 3 to 7 are:

1. **Prioritizing your customers.** Value-based segmentation tells you which customers are valuable and which are less valuable. This allows you to focus on those customers who are of value to your business. You should also focus on making unprofitable customers profitable, which is the equivalent of lowering the horizontal axis. Doing so has the effect of getting the whale a larger body of earnings.

2. **Getting new customers.** Customer analytics can tell you how to get more customers from the same budget and tell you the expected lifetime value of customers acquired through different channels and campaigns.

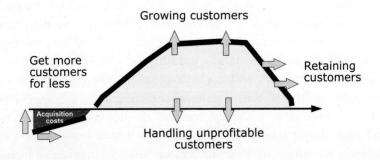

Exhibit 2.7 Four Core Value Disciplines of Sales and CRM

3. **Growing existing customers.** Customer analytics can tell you who to sell what to and when, regardless of whether it is about immediately cross-selling, customer development over time, or wallet share optimization. ("Wallet share" is the percentage of a customer's total spending in your field of business that is awarded to your organization.)

4. **Retaining customers.** Customer intelligence can tell you which customers will leave you and when and why, allowing you to do something about it.

The next sections list some indicators that can help you to identify which sales or CRM value disciplines appear logical to pursue from a strategic perspective. As indicated in Exhibit 2.1, this guidance toward what value disciplines to pursue could serve as first draft for a sales and marketing strategy for stakeholder evaluation. Depending on what is decided, you can then go through the next chapters and pick recipes that support the selected activities and take a business maturity perspective into account. If you need more inspiration, see the case study in Chapter 9. Note that the activities listed in this book should not be seen as mutually exclusive but as ones that can generate synergies to new and already existing processes in your organization at the same time.

In case you want to use the questions presented in the next sections as an interview guide, turn them into a questionnaire. For example, ask: To what extent do you agree with the following statements, where 5 indicates full agreement and 1 indicates that this is not your current strategic situation: Our average earnings per customer is declining. Then you can find the average score for each of the four CRM opportunities and use it for guidance.

Increased Profitability (see Chapter 3)

Value-based segmentation is an essential exercise for all companies. If not for any other reason, it can be used simply to make a long-term strategy focus on valuable segments. Some elements that makes this exercise even more business critical in the short run are listed next.

- Your average earnings per customer is declining.

- You are in a market where historically many discounts have been given and you are dealing with large and complex customers. In this case, customer value estimation can provide you with fact-based input about how to renegotiate contracts and which clauses to update.

- Your earnings per customer are lower than those of your competitors and you are not pursuing a low-cost or extreme growth strategy (since a growth strategy typically is costly).

- You do not know which customers and segments are profitable from an overall company strategic perspective.

- You have customer queuing in your call center or other process and this has a negative effect on the customer loyalty. In such a case, value-based segmentation will help you prioritize your customers.

- You have a plan to introduce a loyalty program. Value-based segmentation will tell you which customers to target and how to graduate customers in the program.

- You are aiming for a retention strategy, since you want to focus on retaining the most valuable customers.

- To follow up on your acquisition strategy: Value-based segmentation can help you identify where and how you have acquired your most valuable customers.

Acquisition Strategy (see Chapter 4)

Most organizations are expected to have acquisition processes. The next list indicates situations in which you or your company should focus even more on these acquisition activities.

- Your objectives clearly indicate that your success is directly linked to your ability to acquire new customers.

- You are placed in sales with no responsibility for what happens after the contract is closed.

- You are strategically positioned in a market with a relatively low penetration compared to expected market potential.

- You have a relatively small customer base according to your strategic ambitions.

- You are introducing new products to the market, and they are not being received well by your existing customer base. An alternative strategy could be to present the product to different market segments from those you historically have approached.

- Your company is pursuing growth via market differentiation and you should enter new markets.

Cross-Selling Strategy (see Chapter 5)

As with acquisition activities, most organizations are expected to have sales processes targeted toward the existing customer base. The next list indicates situations where you or your company should focus even more on these sales activities.

- Your objectives clearly indicate that your success is directly linked to your ability to sell more to your existing customer base.

- You are placed in sales with responsibility for what happens after the contract is closed.

- You have never worked actively with cross-selling and up-selling to your existing customer base. In this case, there are potentially some quick wins here since you already have some customer commitment and trust.

- You are strategically positioned in a market with a relatively high penetration compared to the expected market potential and are in a market with relatively loyal customers.

- You have a relatively large customer base according to your strategic ambitions.

- You are introducing new products to the market, and they are well received by your existing customer base.

- You are responsible for introducing new products into your market. This methodology will give clear input on what bundling offers could be introduced.

- Your company is pursuing growth via product differentiation (adding new products).

Retention Strategy (see Chapter 6)

Many organizations do not have proactive retention activities and rely on complaint handling as a means of customer retention. The next list provides situations where you or your company should increase the focus on retention activities.

- Your objectives clearly indicate that your success is directly linked to your ability to retain existing customers.
- Your customer base is declining either because your market is maturing or your competitiveness is not up to date.
- You are placed in sales with responsibility for what happens after the contract is closed.
- You never before have worked actively with customer retention. There are potentially some quick wins in entering this high-value virgin territory.
- You are strategically positioned in a market with a relatively high penetration rate compared to expected market potential and are in a market with relatively disloyal customers.
- You as a product manager are responsible for introducing new products. This methodology gives clear input on how to design and introduce retention offers.
- Your company is a market leader and pursues growth not through market or product differentiation but through a digging-in strategy.

GENERIC CRM STRATEGY

Even though a generic CRM strategy could seem like a contradiction in terms, we suggest one here. It can serve as starting point or a first draft for your stakeholder interviews. You then can enrich it with specific activities to customize it to your organizational needs. It is based on a value-based segmentation, which in all cases is a logical starting point for all customer analytics activities (see Exhibit 2.8).

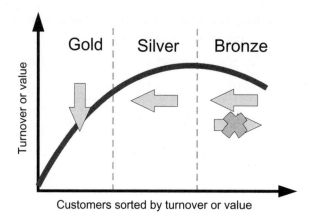

Exhibit 2.8 Generic CRM Strategy Based on Value-Based Segmentation

The strategy simply suggests that you should treat every segment differently and according to its value. The overall idea behind this method is to increase the value of some customers and focus on retaining the most valuable ones. If you cannot grow the customer into becoming valuable, consider terminating the customer relationship since it is destroying value in your business.

Gold customers should be retained even at very high cost simply because they represent very high value. As you already know from the 80-20 rule, they provide the core of your profit. In most cases, reducing their churn by 50% (churn is the percentage of customers that leave you, e.g., per month) can make a company profitable again. This is also described in the case study in Chapter 9. The same results can be found in Frederic Reicheld's book, *The Loyalty Effect*, for different industries.[1]

Silver customers are those who in no way erode your business value but are not critical for the short-term survival of your company. You should seek to make them profitable (gold customers) by increasing their engagement in your business through upgrades, cross-selling, or increasing your wallet shares.

Bronze customers should either be made profitable or dumped. There are several ways of making them profitable.

- Raise prices. After all, you are the ones who sell it cheap to them.
- Reduce service costs (e.g., no more letters, only email).

■ Set them last in queue, which allows you to minimize call center staff only at their expense.

■ Make service-level differentiation and charge them for extra services.

■ Treat them like a discount segment with no frills.

■ Sell them to competitors or daughter companies with more suitable business models.

■ Actively churn these customers, which are eroding your profits.

USING CUSTOMER ANALYTICS AS INSPIRATION FOR A CRM STRATEGY

In the section "From Strategy to Menu," we presented a top-down (strategic) approach to how you can establish a CRM strategy. Market conditions, given objectives, or your role in the organization determines which CRM activities you should pursue. In the section "Generic CRM Strategy" we presented a generic and commonsense approach to how you can prioritize your CRM activities. Here we present a bottom-up (data-driven) approach that is based on trends and movements in the value segments of your customer base and can give indications of what CRM activities you should focus on.

This approach is a natural extrapolation of the generic CRM approach presented earlier, which explained all the basic terms used in Exhibit 2.9 and the logic behind them. The basic idea behind this approach is to track, on a value segment basis, how the profit or turnover is generated between periods. This model therefore gives you an idea about how your customers have moved between value segments since the last period and how successful your acquisition, up-selling and cross-selling, and retention activities have been.

You do not need to have an existing value-based segmentation model to do this analysis. As long as you can allocate the turnover to specific customers and define new and lost customers, you can just define some value segments yourself. For example, a gold customer has a turnover of more than $2,000 per year or period; a bronze customer has a turnover of less than $50 per period; and silver customers fall in between. Of course, make sure that the number and width of

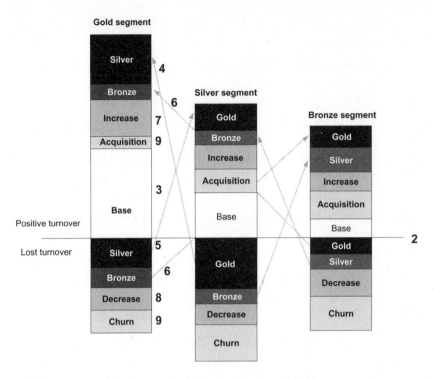

Exhibit 2.9 Parts of the Segment and Turnover Movement Model

the value bands (since you can have more than three) reflects the way your organization today treats its customers and that each value segment has a size that makes it relevant for analysis.

The model is based on nine elements:

1. Three segments: gold, silver, and bronze.

2. A horizontal line that cuts through the bars. What is above the line represents turnover of the segments. The bars below the line represent turnover lost by the segment since the previous period.

3. The bars are made out of nine different areas. The white area represents the base turnover, which is defined as the turnover from customers within each value segment that the same customers also spent in the previous period. Hence, if a customer

spent $90 last year and $110 this year, the $90 goes into the base turnover.

4. The black area above the baseline represents the turnover in the gold segment generated by customers that during the last period were categorized as silver customers. This turnover represents successful cross- and up-selling efforts to silver customers. The turnover movement between the segments is illustrated by a gray line, where each of the areas at the end of the arrows is exactly the same.

5. The black area below the baseline represents turnover that is moved from the gold segment to the silver segment since some customers also have been reallocated to a lower-value segment.

6. There will also be customers moving between the gold and the bronze segment. Since the silver and bronze areas above the horizontal line are larger than the corresponding areas below the line, we can conclude that these movements between the segments have contributed to a growth in the gold segment.

7. The "Increase" area for each of the customer segments is equal to the increased spending of customers that during the last period belonged to the same value segment. Hence if a customer spent $90 last year and $110 this year, the $20 will go into this area.

8. The "Decrease" area represents the opposite of the "Increase" area. If a customer last year spent $90 and this year spent only $70, then the negative difference of $20 would go into this area along with the other entire decreased customer spending. By comparing the Increase and Decrease areas, we learn about the development of spending within the segments.

9. The turnover for each segment can be influenced by the new customer acquisition (above the line) and the customer churn (below the line).

Exhibit 2.10 shows a high-level analysis of the segment and customer movement model. The overall purpose is to get a good understanding of how your customer base evolves by comparing the same colored areas within each of the bars, or by looking at the trends of

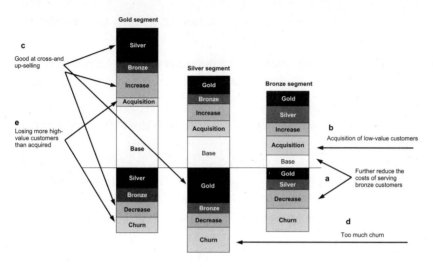

Exhibit 2.10 Analysis of the Segment and Turnover Movement Model

the same colored areas across the bars. If you make this analysis, these developments could be indicated by letters a through e in the exhibit:

a. Can we further reduce the costs of serving the bronze segment without this relatively large decrease in the turnover?

b. Most of the acquisitions fall into the bronze segment, which can indicate that our acquisition processes are targeted toward low-end customers. If this case is confirmed, see Chapter 4 on acquisition processes and learn how you can become better at targeting valuable customers.

c. Indicates that your cross- and up-selling processes to your existing customer base appear to be successful, since there is both a relatively high movement from the silver to the gold segment and because the "Increase" area is larger than the "Decrease" area within the gold and silver segments. You can see this as an opportunity to focus even more on these highly profitable activities. You can read more about how to do this in Chapter 5.

d. There is a lot of churn in the silver segment. This could be a result of many things, ranging from poor treatment of this segment, competition attacks, or a general market. You can read more about how to analyze and react to this situation in Chapter 6.

e. This is also an indication of a potential churn problem, since you are losing more existing gold customers than you are acquiring.

From a data-driven bottom-up perspective, this model can give rise to many hypotheses and lead you toward the CRM activities that appear to be the most relevant for you and your organization. Another strength of this analysis is that it can be replicated down to an individual salesperson or sales department level, which can give good visibility deep into your commercial processes. This means that individuals can be held accountable for the potential success of individual CRM activities.

In many industries, it is very difficult to use a churn definition like the one presented here because customers do not hand in a message defining the final date of their relationship with you. Also, in some industries, there are partial churns, meaning that the customers still continue to buy from you but buy more from your competitors. In such industries, what you define and track as churn can simply be decreased sales.

Not having a clear churn definition also causes some problems with knowing the difference between what was an increased sale to an existing customer and what was a win-back or reacquisition of a previously lost customer. The solution here can be to introduce a churn definition saying that if a customer has purchased nothing for more than 12 months then he will be considered being churned. This means that the same customer can be considered an acquisition if he starts doing business with you again after 13 months. In this case, we would consider:

- **Acquisition (new or won back customers).** The percentage of the total volume or earnings for a given month that is purchased by customers that have been activated for the first time or reactivated after being passive for more than 12 months. In this example, a customer should be considered a new customer for 12 months since it is not until after the first 12 months that we can track up-selling and churn on a customer level.

- **Up-selling (gained wallet share).** The percentage of the total volume or earnings for a given month, aggregated from a customer level, that are purchased in addition to last month's sales, and compared to the same month the year before.

- **Churn (lost wallet share).** The percentage of the total volume or earnings for a given month, aggregated from a customer level, that are purchased less than the previous month, and compared to the same month the year before.

Now you can estimate the acquisition, up-selling, and churn on a monthly basis (which also can serve as key performance indicators) and sum them up for a year (or however long a period you wish), and do the same segment and volume analysis for an industry where customers do not churn through termination of a contract.

FINAL WORD OF ADVICE

If you are responsible for customer intelligence or customer analytics in your organization, one of the most business-critical aspects is to find some good partners in your organization who will be your sponsors. Your sponsors are the people who must support and in the future will make strategic decisions based on your findings. Try to see things from their perspective; there you are with all your vision of data, information, and decision support; why should they trust you? You should prepare properly for your first meetings and never promise more than you can deliver. The golden advice within all information management is: Think big, start small, and deliver quickly. We recommend that you at a minimum make a value-based segmentation or other analysis that can document your value from day 1 to your stakeholders and sponsors. Visions are good, but if you can deliver only on a long-term basis, your stakeholders will lose interest. In addition, you will lose touch and will never be able to implement customer analytics as a strategic asset since you will come nowhere near the strategy creation process.

If you have any questions, you are welcome to contact us via our homepage: www.basm-support.com. Now go to the flowchart in

Exhibit 2.1 and use it for guidance in determining which of the four value disciplines you should pursue as a company. Good luck!

NOTE

1. F. F. Reichheld et al., *The Loyalty Effect: The Hidden Force behind Growth, Profits, and Lasting Value* (Boston, MA: Harvard Business School Press, 1996).

CHAPTER **3**

Lead Information for Identifying Valuable Customers: The Recipe

What if I could tell you how to treat any one of your customers in order to make them all profitable—would that be of interest?

Before you start reading this chapter, you should keep the concept of this book in mind. Chapter 2 is aimed for readers with strategic responsibilities whereas Chapters 3 through 7 are written primarily for project managers and customer analysts. Chapters 1, 8, and 9 are relevant for both user groups. This chapter focuses on where customer analytics becomes reality in the form of concrete analytical methods, data sources, and so on.

We start this chapter by showing some of the activities that you must complete in order to make a customer value estimation, which basically is everything that must occur before you group customers into value-based segments. Customer value estimation is a tool that

41

should be used when doing individual contract negotiations with customers; in contrast, value-based segmentation is an organization-wide standardized way of prioritizing customers. In the second half of this chapter, we show how value-based segmentation can be used as an organization-wide tool for optimizing the way you invest your resources in your customer base.

As demonstrated in Chapter 2 and described next, there are many reasons why you could focus on the estimation of the individual customer value:

- You are in a market where historically many discounts have been given and you are dealing with large and complex customers. Customer value estimation can provide you with fact-based input for negotiations.

- Your average earnings per customer is declining.

- Your earnings per customer are lower than those of your competitors and you are not pursuing a low-cost or extreme growth strategy.

- You do not know which customers and segments are profitable from an overall company strategic perspective.

- You have customer queuing in your call center or in other processes, and this has an effect on their loyalty. Value-based segmentation will help you prioritize them.

- You have or plan to introduce a loyalty program. Value-based segmentation will tell you which customers to target.

- You are aiming for a retention strategy, since you want to focus on retaining the most valuable customers.

- To follow up on your acquisition strategy, value-based segmentation can help you identify where and how you have acquired your most valuable customers.

The first half of the chapter presents a series of generic project steps and project management tools. To minimize the amount of repetition in the book, we present these generic tools and steps only here although we refer to them in later chapters.

CUSTOMER VALUE ESTIMATION FOR NEGOTIATIONS

There are many reasons why customers who look the same are not worth the same amount. This difference in value usually comes down to the way you negotiate contracts or give offers to your customers and the way customers behave.

There are good reasons why rebates should be given during contract negotiations. These reasons could be based on historical delivery errors from your company, competitive pressure, or expected future behavior of the customer. Over time, however, it is hoped that your company will have fewer delivery errors, the competitive price pressure will diminish, and perhaps the behavior promised by your customer is not realized. For these reasons, there are many good grounds for renegotiating given prices.

The value of customers is also a result of how they behave. Perhaps they fax in all their orders instead of using your web order system, which makes them more costly to service. Perhaps they book a lot of slots on your ships and often do not show up with their containers, taking the space from other potential customers. Perhaps they do not want to use direct debit or prepayment, which rolls some financial risk over on your side. Perhaps they call in rather than just following the manual when in doubt. All these behaviors add to your costs. If you do not incentivize customers to change their costly behaviors, they will continue to drive up your costs.

This is what customer value estimation for negotiation is about. It enables you to take fact-based negotiations with your customers on a one-to-one basis and gives you full information as a starting point. If you can document it, the customer cannot deny it. If you can incentivize it well, you should be able to create a win-win situation for both you and the customer. The customer improves his or her behavior and gets rewarded, gives you more or you upgrade service levels, and so on. Over time, this could also mean an increased degree of partnering and integration between your two companies, increasing the length of your business relationship. Customer value estimation should also indicate the results of your improved will and ability to negotiate with your customers; this process monitoring part continuously helps you to select new customers with which to improve your relations.

Project Plan

Exhibit 3.1 shows a high-level project plan where you start from the top and work your way down through it. In the middle there are parallel project activities that require coordination but can be handled at the same time. The rest of this section goes through this project plan step by step.

The first step is to get stakeholder buy-in before you start. Prepare for meetings with your key stakeholders by producing some initial deliverables that prove your skills and indicate the potential value of this project. Chapter 2 provides some strategic arguments. Keep in mind that at the end of the day, these individuals will evaluate your

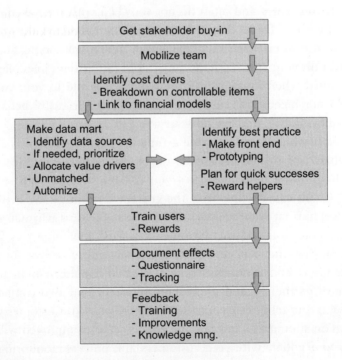

Exhibit 3.1 Project Plan for Customer Value Evaluation

proposal on how it supports their key performance indicators (KPIs), so let that be the basis of your presentation. Try to give them some concrete estimates regarding when you can deliver, what the costs will be, and what outcome you can deliver. You must think like a project manager, which is all about delivering on time, on cost, and on promised quality.

If you work in a large organization, you might go to the procurement department and learn about all the SPSS and SAS licenses in your organization; people who operate these tools often have good insight into what analytical projects could be cooking on the top floor. You could also visit the customer intelligence, the data warehouse (DW), and business intelligence (BI) departments if you are not a part of them. During the project, they will be important stakeholders that have the power to eliminate your project, since they monitor the software and the data accesses.

Mobilizing a team is another important early step in the process. In your initial project plan, you should have an idea about what resources are needed. Your funding should be in place. Now you have to make sure that you have access to all the needed skills and that managers sign off indicating their willingness to let personnel participate in the project. If you cannot get access to the required skills or needed funding, go back to your stakeholders and ask for support. If this does not help you, either abandon the project or get another sponsor. Create a proper kickoff for the project, which increases the commitment between all involved parties.

When you have your team in place, you might find that there is a long list of stakeholders that you will need to approach, ranging from the team members, their managers, and other individuals. At this point you should consider creating a stakeholder map, such as the one shown in Exhibit 3.2.

The stakeholder map gives you input about how you should communicate to all your stakeholders, where conflicts could arise, and also hints about how stakeholders might interact internally when you are not in the room. In Exhibit 3.2, there could be a risk that the information technology (IT) department will contact your BI department at some point and convince it formally or informally that your projects should be closed down or perhaps handed over to the BI department.

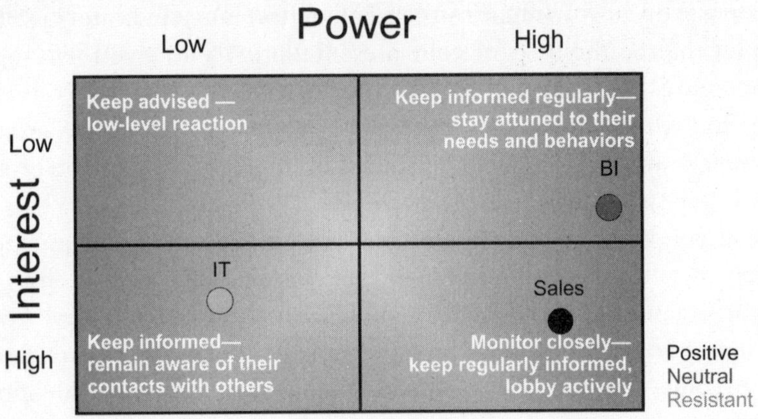

Exhibit 3.2 Stakeholder Map

This could be the case if the IT department for some reason supports your project but has to work through others in order to have an effect. The arguments used could be about IT governance or the data architecture; whether they are right or wrong, you should handle the problem up front. If not, you can expect that the BI department will suddenly take an interest in your project while representing your IT department's viewpoint. The stakeholder map can be combined with the level of conflict model presented in the pages to follow.

Identifying all relevant cost drivers is a critical success factor for your project. Your focus should be on the cost drivers that you can negotiate with customers. As mentioned, these include discounts compared to list or average prices. They are also the costs that the customer inflicts on your company via its behavior. Elements that are not controlled by your customer are irrelevant for this negotiation tool.

Keep in mind that you are not supposed to know everything yourself. Therefore, you or the members of your project team can get information about cost drivers by interviewing members of the rest of the organization. Try to be creative when you suggest how your organization can reward customers for changing behavior, which essentially will be an additional parameter used to negotiate.

Most likely one of your key stakeholders will be your finance department. Make sure that the data you use is aligned with its data.

Try to align your model with whatever financial controlling tools are in place. This is not about taking over the jobs of members of the finance department; it is about not creating another version of the truth where you say that a customer is profitable and finance rejects this idea.

To make a data mart, your project requires specialist skills and specialist tools. As a starting point, we recommend tools like Base SAS or SPSS modeler. If you believe that you have found a better tool, be aware of these selection criteria:

- The tool should be produced by vendors that you expect will exist in the market in the future.
- The vendor should be able to provide training in how to use the tools in the start-up phase as well as providing future training to new employees due to job rotation.
- The tool should be easy to install on a standard PC. Do not go for big and costly server solutions unless there are very strong arguments for doing so.
- The tool should have integrated database connectivity, which allows you to automate the data sourcing using standard technology.
- The tool should be easy to upgrade with data-mining and other analytical functionalities.
- The tool should allow for quick, complex data manipulation.
- The tool should allow you to automate the data management process.

Do not use Access and Excel for these kinds of jobs. They do not have the flexibility or ability to scale out to large data sets, and are not useful analytical tools—they are the tools of analytical *amateurs*. This might change in the future, but this is the status as of this writing. If you already know for sure that you will not do data mining on the data and your data sets are relatively simply to manipulate, you can consider standard BI server technology.

The next step is to identify data sources, which can be a more or less cumbersome task depending on how professionally your IT and DW departments are organized. If you find that many data sources

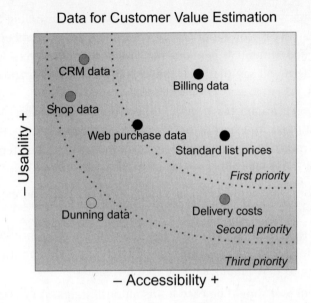

Exhibit 3.3 Data Sources Plotted According to Their Accessibility and Usability

are accessible and usable to varying degrees, you can put them in a plot and prioritize their sourcing, as shown in Exhibit 3.3.

The level of data granularity needed reflects how you can allocate the costs and how the end user's process is designed. In the logistical industry, you might want to present the information on a "per send item type" level, since negotiators want to be able to break down data per import and export location, cargo type, and so on. In the telecom industry, this data mart might contain only one line per customer or subscription and then one variable for each identified and controllable cost driver. In general, however, you should keep the granularity level at the lowest manageable level since the data foundation might change over time as the IT landscape or strategy changes, and also because doing so will make this data foundation useful for other purposes in the future. Remember, you can always aggregate up.

If you have to combine data from different information systems, you will often find that the data does not match on a one-to-one basis. You may find that 5% of the data is unmatched. In this case you should not necessarily be worried since in most cases a decision maker with 5% uncertainty would make the decision anyway, and in all cases he or she is better off than if there had been no decision support available. You should, however, document this for the training session in the implementation phase so that end users know the risks of making decisions on marginal differences. You also should consider whether the unmatched amounts should be neglected or, more likely, should be evenly allocated to all the customer's activities in order for your data mart to deliver the same bottom-line result as the one you find other places in the organization, such as finance; remember, you must have one version of the truth, or you might destroy the trust in your tool. You should not neglect data sources of poor quality; only through documenting the consequences of poor data quality will someone do something about it. If you neglect poor data quality, the problem will not go away; it will only be passed to the next project that needs the data.

It is also important that you think in terms of automating the data process. Doing so is not necessary in the prototype phase, when you are building the data mart for the first time, but it will become important at a later stage when you put the data processes into production. This way you ensure that the good developers (and only the good ones can do stuff like this within a reasonable time frame) do not get stuck with maintaining their own solutions; you can leave maintenance to the next line of analysts or data managers. Another advantage of automating the process is that when you minimize the level of human intervention, you also minimize the risk of human errors. Always try, therefore, from day one to think in terms of automating the data flow in combination with data quality checkpoints that expose irregularities in the data. A simple example of how you automate data processes could be via copying the SQL that is generated in your front-end tool, such as, copying business objects into your data management program. Also remember to make the documentation as you go along and to check and document unmatched amounts after all the data mergers.

Identifying best practices is one of the fastest ways of creating value when improving processes. It is also important to understand that you should never "just" create a technical solution and expect people to figure it out by themselves. If you want to gain the full potential from your technical solution, you must train the users. How

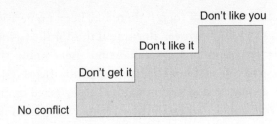

Exhibit 3.4 Levels of Conflict (Can Be Combined with Your Stakeholder Map)

else would you expect everyone to use it in the optimal way from day one? Also, keep in mind that you are asking people to change the way they work and that changing behavior is not something people do unless they can see clear benefits in doing so. If people do not understand why they should change, they will not like your project. If you continue to put pressure on them, they will stop liking *you*, and suddenly you have created a conflict. As soon as you are gone, they will go back to doing things as they always have done (see Exhibit 3.4). Also you will find that you are less welcome the next time around when you introduce a project.

When you have identified what you believe is the best practice, and if you believe it cannot be improved further for now, you should start designing the front end system for your users. As discussed in Chapter 1, there are basically two types of information: lead and lag information, or information that you act on in new ways and information that you use to monitor the results of your actions. The next step is to go to your end users and ask which information they require and how it should be presented in order for them to prepare themselves for the negotiations and to see whether things have improved afterward from their perspective.

The salesperson might simply require a data dump in Excel (here used as a front end tool, not the data generation system), which shows customer trends over the last periods and possibly some visualization to support the overview. Perhaps it also includes an indicator of whether the different cost drivers are unusual for the specific customer in order for the salesperson to pick up on extreme differences. Exhibit 3.5 shows what could be a first draft for the salespeople to work by. The salespeople might come up with another solution, and

Exhibit 3.5 First Draft for a Report

	200801	200802	200803	200804	200805	200806	200807	200808	200809	200810	200811	200812	Average	Bench.
Turnover	100%	100%	100%	100%	100%	100%	100%	100%	100%	100%	100%	100%	100%	100%
Cost A	8%	7%	8%	8%	11%	13%	23%	15%	16%	19%	30%	17%	14%	5%
CostB	2%	2%	2%	3%	3%	5%	3%	2%	4%	2%	8%	2%	3%	2%
Cost C	8%	8%	7%	7%	8%	10%	12%	9%	8%	9%	16%	6%	8%	7%
Cost D	16%	13%	12%	12%	13%	15%	19%	13%	14%	14%	26%	13%	14%	16%
Cost E	37%	30%	29%	27%	30%	33%	39%	26%	26%	28%	41%	26%	30%	20%
Cost F	1%	2%	3%	2%	3%	4%	3%	3%	4%	5%	3%	2%	3%	6%
Profit	27%	38%	41%	43%	32%	21%	2%	32%	28%	23%	-23%	33%	28%	44%
KPI	61%	85%	92%	97%	73%	47%	4%	73%	64%	52%	-53%	75%	63%	100%
Bonus/$	610	854	919	965	726	471	38	726	644	518	-529	752	629	

together you can develop the information tool that supports their personal objectives. You could even consider redesigning the way you reward your sales staff and show it in the tool in order to motivate use of the tool.

Exhibit 3.5 shows a simple example of how a customer-specific report could look. The report is made for a period of 12 months and shows the turnover in percent minus six individual cost drivers. The average column indicates that costs A and E with 14% and 30% are well over the average costs of 5% and 20% (benchmark). The salesperson can also read that he or she will get only 63% of the average bonus for that particular customer. From this, the salesperson should be incentivized to go on a customer visit and discuss how to minimize these costs or discounts. It is important for you to understand and respect that the end users very often themselves do not know exactly what they want. For this reason, you should expect a prototyping process, such as the one presented in Exhibit 3.6, to go on for several iterations.

When you have finalized prototyping the optimal front end for all your different user groups, keep in mind that sales managers might want to have an overview across all the customers they are responsible for, and top management might want to break it down on product types and segments, and so on.

The next technical element you should consider is the information architecture, which has to do with how you intend to transport the right data to the right people. Will you email the Excel sheets? Will you make a web front end where people can extract the data themselves? Will all salespeople get an application on their laptop so they slice and dice offline? If so, how will you install and maintain that application?

The last leg of the technical front end solution is to tie up all ends from getting the data from your data mart to the users and making the information available in the desired format with the desired functionalities in terms of interactivity, security, layout, and graphics. This is also called your technology strategy; your aim is to get the right technical software and hardware tied together into one coherent process. This process should be cost effective to set up and maintain while at the same time able to deliver the requested decision support.

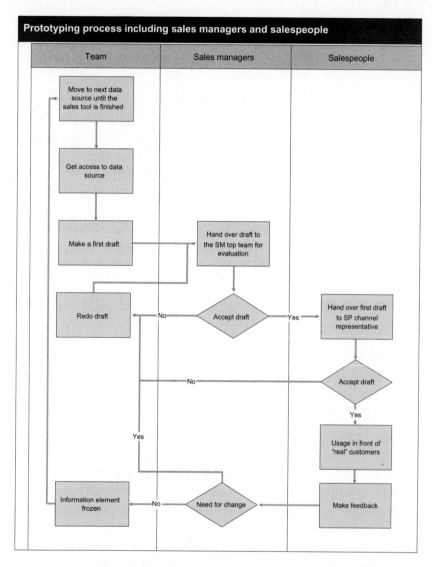

Exhibit 3.6 Process Map Describing a Prototyping Process with Unclear User Requirements

Plan for Quick Success

When you implement new information tools, you should plan for quick successes for three reasons:

1. **To maintain your stakeholder support.** Your stakeholders have been betting on you. You must now show them that they put their money on the right horse. Perhaps other projects that you were on were canceled before they were fully rolled out; of course, this is something you wish to avoid. Again, you must see the situation from your stakeholders' point of view. If they are placed highly in the organization, they work through others, and they will and should focus on the persons who have the ability to deliver on time, on cost, and on quality. To do so, they will use indicators like early successes as benchmarks.

2. **For your training program.** This is where you must convince users that what you are training them for is a better method; they cannot argue with success.

3. **If you cannot produce some quick successes, you might have gotten it all wrong.** Perhaps you were set up for failure from day one; perhaps you did not find best practices. Whatever the reason, you should reconsider your rollout. Many project managers can deliver what they have been told to, but only the best can deliver successes.

If you are using storytelling to exemplify how things have been done successfully, you will have a very good opportunity to reward those people who supported you from day one by mentioning their names or using them in training sessions. This also gives you the opportunity to signal that you will reward people for participating in future projects.

Train Users

If you have followed this project plan, it should be clear to you that the training session should not be focused on the technical solution but on the identified best practice of how to do things, and how the front end of the technical solution can enable users to realize these best practices.

You should also have prepared some success stories that show users they will be rewarded for adapting to the ways of working presented.

Our research has showed that when employees in successful companies are faced with changes in the competitive environment, they have the ability to identify and use information in response to those changes. If you work for such an information-proactive organization, you as a trainer should be humble and continue to listen and learn how to improve the process either because of changes in the business environment or because of the innovation happening around you. Our research also shows that if you want people to feel in control of their working lives, you must, among other things, give them some objectives that they directly can influence. Therefore, you should include the incentive strategy in the training program to enable individuals or groups to identify what is in it for them.

When you train people in how to use a technical solution, you should focus on three elements:

1. **Data quality.** Users should be confident about making decisions based on the existing data quality. If there are issues with the data quality, people should be informed about how this can effect their decisions. This is important, since you often find that people who are not properly trained hesitate about making obvious decisions, even though the data quality is only about 1% off and this 1% will not impact what is a right decision.

2. **Support and training.** These should always be available. You should make sure that people know where to go if they get stuck at some point. Also consider how new users arriving after the tool's rollout should be trained and registered as users.

3. **User-friendliness.** Users should find the tool to be user-friendly in the way it supports their way of working. This is why you should identify best practices first and design the front end afterward.

Monitor the Usage and Impact of the Tool

After a project has been implemented, it will be handed over to the new process owners. For them to be able manage the new process,

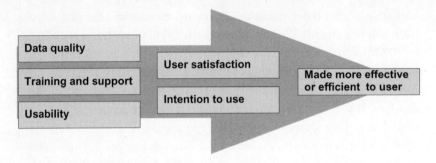

Exhibit 3.7 Simplified DeLone Model

you should give them some indicators of the user satisfaction and the usage. User satisfaction can be measured relatively objectively via a questionnaire focusing on the whole new process or just the technical customer analytics tool, depending on your focus. If the focus is on the whole process, the questionnaire should be structured according to the different process steps. If the focus is on the technical solution, a DeLone model can be used (see Exhibit 3.7). This model tells you that users are interested in high data quality, good training and support, and high usability. If they are satisfied with all of these elements, they will use (or intend to use) the tool. But the ultimate question is whether the tool has made them make better decisions and/or helps them spend fewer resources on getting to the point where they can make the decisions. Since that is where the value creation for the organization is, you have to ask users about this also.

An alternative to questionnaires are system measurements of usage. These could include web logs that on a monthly basis tell you whether one particular customer report has been requested every month or whether usage is following your prescribed best practice. If you find that some of your sales staff has stopped using the reports, you can immediately investigate why and act on this. After all, institutionalizing a best practice is the same as changing their job description. They will have to make very persuasive arguments to justify how they can both accept their salary and not do their jobs at the same time.

Creating Feedback Processes

Feedback processes can be used for improving existing processes, including how training and support is handled and the technical solution itself. Feedback processes do not have to be aimed at the process owner alone but can also be aimed toward other users. This is often referred to as knowledge management, which means storing knowledge for later use.

The purpose of knowledge management is the same as writing a book: It is to make individual perishable competencies generic and shared sustainable competencies. Knowledge management therefore deals with capturing what works and what does not and sharing it with others. This can be done via training sessions, or it can be via monthly reports entered into a template about what went right or wrong during the last customer negotiations and then uploaded in a database or an intranet community. Other users of the same or related processes can search on how to handle negotiations on different cost elements, read about how other salespersons did, or possibly even contact them.

Other Considerations

In large organizations, you might find that the front ends and information needs are very different according to where the individual users are placed in an organization. (See Exhibit 3.8.)

Exhibit 3.8 Pyramid of Different Kinds of Decision Makers

Starting from the bottom of the pyramid, these different information needs could be:

- Local sales reps will need operational information as input for their customer negotiations. The information types are lead information to act on and lag information, which helps reps monitor the effects.

- Local sales managers who perhaps only lead others will also require lead and lag information; however, its format should be different. Lead information typically is in plots or comparisons that indicate which customers or customer types are creating the least value, along with indicators of why, for further investigation. Lag indicators also focus on which sales reps should be rewarded for increasing the value of the customer base, while other sales reps should be trained to do the same. The sales manager should also be given an indication of the aggregated effects of the negotiations as a key performance indication. In order for the manager to monitor success, he or she potentially could be allowed to compare the progress with one of the other sales managers.

- From a center perspective, data-mining techniques can be very useful in providing an overall picture of the characteristics of those customers who are more or less profitable. You have to keep in mind that sales reps with 20 customers in a local organization might not be able to see the patterns based on their few customers in relation to the full customer base. An example could be if you learned that customers acquired during the price war of 2008 are unprofitable. This could be an insight that some, but not all, of the local sales managers identified. In this case, it would be a logical move from the center to identify the critical customers on a list and send it to the sales managers with some clear targets, and some informational material for the sales reps and campaign material for the customers. This way the center can also proactively support the sales processes continuously in how to become more efficient from a holistic perspective rather than just telling sales to increase the sales target 10% on a yearly basis. Lag information would, as always, mirror the lead information; in this example it would be the increased profitability of the customer segment acquired during 2008.

If this is the first project of its kind in your organization, you should consider quick wins with other departments. Perhaps you could make a tool for all the sales offices that indicates how profitable they are, including all the costs that they can control, like cost of housing, head counts, and so on. The benefit for the whole organization would be to improve its general decision-making processes based on financial information from a holistic perspective where everyone is accountable for the costs they control. All of this information would be presented in a central data mart, providing the organization with one version of the truth. Yet you must remember the golden rule: "Think big, start small, and deliver quickly," which means that even though you are keeping the needs of other departments in mind, this should not obstruct your project; it just means that your project will enable and prepare for some later opportunities.

CUSTOMER VALUE ESTIMATION FOR VALUE-BASED SEGMENTATION

Customer value estimation for negation basically means that the knowledge we have about the value of our customers is being used more or less only within the sales department. Very often and for very good reasons, this knowledge is also used for organization-wide purposes, such as prioritizing customers when they are queuing or given different offerings, for strategy planning, when sales ownership has to be defined, when different service levels must be set, and so on. Therefore, there are several differences between customer value estimation and value-based segmentation:

- Value-based segmentation includes all costs that can be allocated to a customer, not just the ones that the sales department can control.
- Value-based segmentation is based not on value alone; often it is combined with input regarding the strategic importance of the customer, credit risks, and other business rules.

■ Value-based segmentation is centrally governed by a customer relationship management (CRM), sales, or marketing department in order for it to be owned by a department that is close to the customers and is interested in optimizing the total customer lifetime value across the whole customer base.

Another argument for a central ownership of the value-based segmentation is based on the fact that customers, regardless of their interaction point and when they interact, should get consistent treatment. The alternative of allowing the different functions to make their own way of prioritizing customers is simply not appropriate because customers will be treated inconsistently, which means that goodwill developed in one process will be destroyed in another. Finally, you will eliminate duplicate efforts in your organization if you decide to act on only one shared value-based "segmentation" or "customer prioritization" model.

From a strategic perspective, a value-based segmentation also adds a new tool for those implementing strategic projects. They now can start configuring processes adapted to the most valuable customers instead of just to customer needs. This could give you some very essential ingredients for the marketing strategy since strategizing primarily deals with configuring what you offer in a way that maximizes that long-term value of your current and future customer base. In the next sections we show how different functions can make use of value-based segmentation. The sum of all these ways, and whatever other ways you can think of, is the building blocks of how you can configure your market offer. These are the elements that you must put together in the right way to create your winning formulas enabled through customer analytics.

From a project manager perspective, the overall flow of the project will be the same when you do an organization-wide rollout of a value-based segmentation model as illustrated in Exhibit 3.9. Instead of rolling it out only in the sales function, you will now have to take other functions into account. After the implementation, the process that you will be responsible for typically will be just to make sure that a new segmentation procedure is executed every month and uploaded in a central DW, where all the individual functions can extract the data needed for their applications and processes. You will, of course,

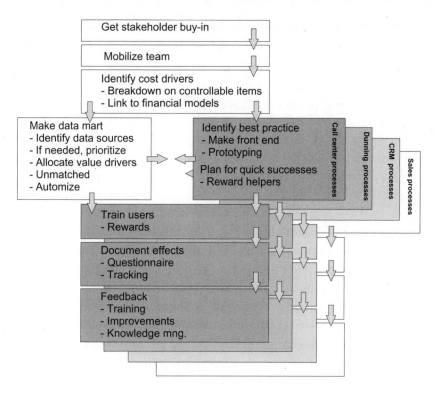

Exhibit 3.9 Value-Based Segmentation Project Plan for More Functions

need to sign off on the model with more parties, yet the individual functions typically set up their own procedures, applications, and training programs.

CRM

In Chapter 2 we showed why value-based segmentation is one of the most essential tools within customer analytics since all other activities, including the overall CRM strategy, will be based on it. This is why the CRM department should own the value-based segmentation—this department is the primary user of value-based segmentation.

In brief, we showed in Chapter 2 that:

■ Retention activities should focus on the most valuable customers (see also Chapters 6 and 9).

- Cross- and up-selling activities should be targeted at the less valuable customers in order to grow their value (see also Chapter 5).

- Customers who destroy value should be forced into becoming valuable. Should they leave your business during this process, that would represent a gain for you (see the beginning of this chapter and Chapter 2 for more details).

Very often CRM departments are in charge of customer loyalty programs, which typically means investing in your best customers in order to grow and retain them. Value-based segmentation, as it has been presented thus far, has been based on the value that the customer has to you as a company. If, however, you go out in the open and nominate a group of customers as gold, silver or bronze customers, very often you will be forced into using turnover-based segmentation or some other criterion that is easy to communicate to customers and for them to understand. Since the customers now know why they belong to each segment, it will also become easier for them to change their behavior in a manner that upgrades them to a higher segment or helps them maintain their current status, which is one of the main reasons for going out in the open with a loyalty program.

Loyalty cards and programs are potentially very strong tools for your CRM programs in business areas where you otherwise have no information about customers' buying habits. This is not the case in the telecommunication, insurance, financial industry, or the "Internet login" industry where you can easily link transactional data to the subscription. It is, however, the case for supermarkets, clothing stores, and the like. The issuance of a card tells us who customers are and how we can get in contact with each on a one-to-one basis. If customers use this card during visits to any one of your stores, you will be able to save this information about customer behavior centrally. An example is a supermarket chain that from the customer registration process knows how many individuals are in the cardholder's family and also registers how many calories are bought within its outlets. This allows the chain to estimate the "share of stomach" as a measure of whether the card holder must be shopping elsewhere in order to feed the whole family. If a customer shops elsewhere, you can estimate which products are bought elsewhere by comparing the shopping basket to a typical shopping basket for that particular customer segment. Now you can communicate relevant offers on a one-to-one basis as they are introduced in the local stores. This information also can be used as lead information for campaigns on a shop level if the statistics shows that milk typically is bought elsewhere.

Another example is from the furniture industry, where customers have to register to get an expensively produced product catalog yet lose the right to this catalog if they do not purchase anything from the furniture vendor for a certain period. Customers also will get email offers on the same style of sofas three to five years after their last purchase, depending on the expected lifetime of the product.

Loyalty programs also provide you with good opportunities for differentiating your business on the business-to-consumer market. At one point I worked for Orange, an urban telecommunication brand primarily known in Europe. Gold customers were given a loyalty card as a token of their status and were also invited to rock concerts, fancy cafés, action movies, and many other activities "with an urban edge." Later I created a similar program for another telecommunication operator, which was one of the old players in the market with an older customer base. Hence the program offered customers tickets to family concerts, family restaurants, video rentals, and so on. In this way the loyalty card was also branding the telecommunication companies since what was promoted via the loyalty programs strongly supported the customers' brand perception.

Sales

Value-based segmentation is also one of the primary tools in the business-to-business market for selecting which customers should get access to their own key client manager, who should use the call center, who can negotiate for discounts, and so on. Hence value-based segmentation becomes a central tool that dictates ownership of individual customers.

Value-based segmentation will also support your acquisition processes by allowing you to identify which campaigns and channels give you the most valuable customers. After all, acquisition campaigns are like fishing with a net; you get some big fish and you get some small fish, and you probably should stop fishing the places where the catch does not pay off. By using value-based segmentation for campaign evaluation, you can also avoid situations where the sales department gets many customers of little value but is still rewarded because the department's bonus system is based on the number, not the quality, of the customers acquired. Value-based segmentation can get you out of a situation where you pay a lot for something that is worthless.

Strategy

Strategy basically deals with two objectives: levering short-term issues and gaining long-term competitive advantages. In both cases, value-based segmentation and customer value estimation are essential.

In situations where short-term issues have to be addressed from a strategic level and these issues are related to the way you treat your customers, value-based segmentation will give you clear indicators of which customers must suffer until you get your overall service delivery up to a level where it is not a strategic issue anymore.

As part of long-term strategizing, very often many needs-based segmentation efforts are combined with the expected growth rates per segment. Customer value estimation provides you with the essential input about which segments are profitable and which are not. If you do not include the value parameter into your strategizing efforts, you will be guided by growth only in terms of turnover and not profitability, which can be a dangerous cocktail in industries where big customers are given big discounts. Alternatively, if you do not consider the customer value at all, you might try to satisfy the needs of all your segments, which is known as "death by being stuck in the middle," because you often are too unfocused and therefore too expensive in what you offer to the market. Your brand could also lose its penetration power because you will end up as a Jack of all trades and master of none.

Finance

It is obvious that if you pursue profitable growth as a strategic parameter, you will also be inclined to implement an organization-wide value-based segmentation model to implement this growth strategy. In this case, the strategy controllers in your finance department will need to make reporting based on your value-based segmentation since growth in the gold segment is good and growth in the bronze segment is less so. If you do not break down your reports by value segments, your controllers will not be able to monitor your strategic success.

Fraud detection and risk management should also be managed according to value-based segmentation. If, for instance, you have an issue with an "old" high-value customer, you could consider calling him or her or applying a "softer" dunning procedure in order to reward historic good behavior. After all, the mantra of CRM—"You know what you have got in your customer base, you do not know what you get through acquisition"—reminds us that it is cheaper to hold onto a gold customer than it is to go out and acquire a new one.

Call Centers

Value-based segmentation can be used in call centers. However, the same logic would apply to all processes that include queuing, whether it is containers that have to wait for the next ship, broken windows that have to be repaired, or goods that have to be delivered.

It would also apply to getting access to offers. If you are a regular customer in a store and it has winter sales with 70% discounts on selected items, you should not queue on equal terms with other people who shop there only for the winter sales.

Prioritizing Customers

Call centers are functional departments where the ability to have the right amount of agents at the right time is key. If you have more agents than needed, you are running too costly an operation. If you have too few, you will create customer dissatisfaction because of increased wait time. There are many ways you can optimize the number of agents, ranging from analytically forecasting to having people doing something else in the nonpeak hours. Whatever way you go about it, once in a while there will be queuing and user dissatisfaction about it.

If you are a commercial organization, you should consider different queuing scenarios for different customer types. It may be that the queuing line is sorted simply by value segment, meaning that gold customers always jump the queue while bronze customers simply will have to call in later. Alternatively, you could make one queue per segment and differentiated waiting times (e.g., gold customers wait a maximum of 30 seconds, silver customers a maximum of 2 minutes, and bronze customers a maximum of 8 minutes).

Educating Customers

In call centers, there are also times of internal overcapacity. During such times we can, at no cost, start educating our customers in ways that make them more profitable and potentially increase their satisfaction, if they, for example, learn to solve their problems via a web page. Earlier it was mentioned that cross- and up-selling activities typically should be aimed toward the silver and bronze segments. Practically this could mean that if a call center agent sees that the waiting time for customers calling in is less than, for example, 30 seconds and there is a silver customer on the phone, the agent can start doing cross-selling. Alternatively, if it is a bronze customer, the agent can train the customer in how to use self-service on the web rather than calling in; and so on.

CHAPTER 4

Lead Information: What You Need to Know before Launching New Acquisition Activities

If I told you where and how you optimally could get your new customers, would that be of any interest to you?

This chapter is about how you can use customer analytics to improve your acquisition processes. This can be done in many ways, depending on the maturity of your information systems. That there is a relationship between which types of acquisition processes you can do and the information you have available should come as no surprise if you picture two organizations, one with a data warehouse (DW) and one without. In this case the organization with a DW would continuously be able to track the quality of new customers per campaign or channel, whereas the other organization would have to rely on beliefs or occasional studies assumed to be representative for all new customers. Because this relationship between the type of information that you have available and acquisition activities that you can do is essential, you can use the guide in the beginning of this chapter to lead you directly to the section of most relevance to you. Each of these sections then focuses on the relationship between data and analytical methodology, and how you can integrate the results into the way you do business. For more complex projects, the chapter also briefly describes the order in which things should be done. If you would like to read more about change management, stakeholder management, conflict resolution, and so on, read the first half of Chapter 3 as inspiration.

Either you are reading this book from one end to the other or you are reading this chapter because Chapter 2 recommended that you do so. This chapter focuses on how customer analytics can support your organization in getting new customers. Strategic reasons for focusing on acquisition processes may include:

- Your objectives clearly indicate that your success is directly linked to your ability to acquire new customers.
- You are placed in sales with no responsibility for what happens after the contract is closed.
- You are strategically positioned in a market with a relatively low penetration compared to expected market potential.
- You have a relatively small customer base according to your strategic ambitions.
- You are introducing new products to the market and they are not well received by your existing customer base.
- Your company is pursuing growth via market differentiation (entering new markets).

There might be other reasons for embarking on acquisition initiatives, since the acquisition of new customers typically is simply something that companies have to do on a continuous basis. Alternatively, perhaps your marketing strategy has up-prioritized customer acquisition activities, which could be a strategic objective of maintaining your position in a market where customers are very hard to retain. Possibly you do not have a budget for retention activities or you do not know who your customers are and for this reason cannot opt for a retention strategy. Perhaps you want to rebuild a new customer base because

Start here

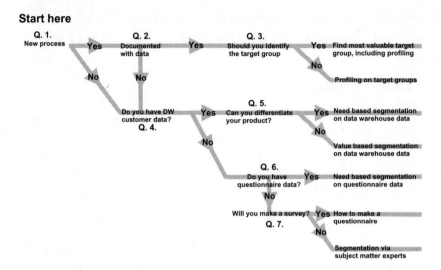

Exhibit 4.1 Chapter Structure

of a strategy change. This chapter guides you on how to use analytics, given your present position.

The decision diagram presented in Exhibit 4.1 could be drawn in many other ways. This perspective was chosen since it depends on your organizational information system maturity, which is described in more detail in Chapter 8. This maturity perspective will not only indicate how you should do customer analytics today, but it also will show tomorrow's opportunities.

This chapter is about how you work with and generate *lead* information *before* creating a new acquisition process. The concept of lead information was described in Chapter 1. In brief, however, lead information describes the type of information that you as a commercial department require in order to take your sales processes to the next level.

You should also read Chapter 7, which focuses on how to create and work with *lag* information. (Lag information is distinct in the sense that it is used to monitor and optimize within the framework of an existing process.) Lag information is something you work with in campaigns during their execution. Finally, you should also read Chapter 8 about *learning* information, which explains how you can use customer analytics systematically to improve your organizational skills *after* a campaign has been finalized.

BEFORE YOUR CAMPAIGN

This section describes a series of analytical options, based on the series of assumptions closely linked to your objectives and the maturity of your organization. In general, customer analytics is heavily associated with business intelligence and use of data warehouse data. In this chapter we also discuss the use of subject matter expert and question-naire data as a means of making a segmentation model, simply *because customer analytics should not be defined by where the data comes from but by the type of decision support that the data enables.* See Chapter 1 for a more detailed discussion. This chapter promotes different analytically derived methodologies, used at different times, with no limitation on where the data is sourced; while still promoting a path that will mature your information systems. You can either choose to read the full chapter for inspiration, or you can go to parts of the chapter that you find most relevant. Exhibit 4.1 can show you where to go, if you choose to go directly to a specific section. Start using the decision tree in the upper left corner. Based on your response to the seven ques-tions, you will get direction about what is likely to be relevant for you. The seven questions are:

1. **Is it an existing business process?** The purpose of this ques-tion is to uncover whether this acquisition campaign is some-thing you have done before. If this is a completely new process, there cannot be any historical data to support your analytical efforts. If it is a known process, you might have a lot of perfor-mance data to learn from. If it is a currently ongoing campaign, also read Chapter 7 for more information.

2. **If this is not a new process, does data exist about the process?** If the answer is no, from a customer analytics per-spective you are as well off as if you had to establish this process for the first time. If the answer is yes, there might exist some usable lag information describing campaign performance that can support your analytical efforts and may be turned into lead information.

3. **Is picking the most valuable campaign among a series of alternatives part of the assignment, or do you wish to optimize a given campaign/acquisition process?**

4. **Do you have access to DW data?** Even though we do not have any historical data on the specific acquisition processes that we can work with, we are still interested in using DW information if it is available. If the answer is yes, we will work on different ways of selecting and generating target groups based on DW information.

5. **Can you differentiate you product?** How we define our target groups also has to do with whether we can differentiate our offer according to customer needs or whether we simply want to prioritize our efforts according to whom we believe will be the most valuable customers in the future.

6. **Do you have questionnaire data?** If there is no DW information available, we still might have some questionnaire information that we can reuse for segmentation purposes.

7. **Will you make a survey?** If not, you can choose to make a questionnaire or you can interview subject matter experts within the organization in order to create a segmentation model. These interviews can also serve as a first step in creating a questionnaire that confirms a conceptual segmentation model.

FINDING THE MOST VALUABLE TARGET GROUP

This section was written for processes owners who want to optimize existing acquisition activities and who have DW information about which customers historically were acquired through which campaigns. The aim of this section is to show how you can identify which campaigns are the most valuable for your company from a return on investment (ROI) perspective.

We do not explain how to profile customer groups until the next section, but it is a logical next step. We separate profiling into an independent section because the methodology used for profiling has no resemblance to value estimation. Also, profiling often is done as a stand-alone exercise. These two analytical approaches do, however, supplement each other well.

When you are executing acquisition activities, obviously you do not know the value of the customers you will get out of the campaign. If you can identify customer segments similar to the ones that you expect to acquire, since it is a relaunch of a campaign, you will be able to estimate the "customer lifetime value" of the potential new customers. You can estimate the lifetime value of a customer or a group of customers by using the formula that was presented in the whale model in Chapter 2:

Acquisition costs per customer − (Average earnings per customer per time unit × Average lifetime)

The three elements of the formula are:

1. **Expected acquisition costs.** They can be estimated as the total campaign costs divided by the number of customers acquired from the campaign. In the information wheel presented in Chapter 1 and Chapter 8, you can read about knowledge management, which means storing overall learning for later use, for others doing parallel activities in other countries or business units, and for your strategy department. If you have stored historical campaign knowledge, you can use it to estimate acquisition costs. Alternatively you can consult specialists in the field or simply rely on your own guesswork.

2. **Expected average value.** You can estimate this based on your customer value estimation (see Chapter 3). If you use questionnaire input, you should be aware that the customers only can report their spending, which means that you have to deduct the variable costs for the particular segment.

3. **Expected average lifetime.** You can estimate this based on survival statistics from your DW. This cannot be done simply by estimating, on average, how long a customer maintains its paying relationship. It is not possible to estimate the average customer lifetime for a group of customers before the last one has churned since the last customer will also affect the total average up until the very last day. This is where survival statistics (i.e., Kaplan-Meyer) come in handy. As the name indicates,

this analytical method has its origin in the medical world, where different medicine was given to groups of patients and the average survival time after taking the medicine was estimated. This statistical method was invented because researchers cannot wait for all the patients to reach their final age, simply because many would survive whatever they were treated for. From a data perspective, all you need are three variables:

a. Is it still an active customer (yes or no)?

b. How long has been or was the customer active for?

c. Which campaign acquired the customer?

This way of testing also allows you to create a special test that identifies whether customers from one campaign typically leave early in the relationship with your organization (customers that only wanted the welcoming gift) or whether they stay significantly longer into the later part of the relationship (long-term relational customers).

Exhibit 4.2 presents the customer lifetime of two campaigns. When the customers started their relationship with the organization, they all became active customers, as shown; at day one, 100% of the customers are active. Over time, we find that the curve for the customers acquired through campaign B is steeper than the curve for the customers acquired through campaign A. To be more precise, after approximately 1.4 years, 50% of customers acquired through campaign B have churned and after approximately 2.4 years, 50% of customers acquired through campaign A have churned. Be aware that

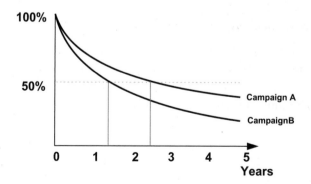

Exhibit 4.2 Survival Statistics

the average customer lifetime will be longer than the 1.4 and 2.4 years since the 50% mark represents the median (the middle observation in a sorted set) and the curve is not linear but concave. The two numbers therefore represent the median customer lifetime. However, the average customer lifetime can also be estimated by most analytical software at 95% confidence intervals.

This way of estimating the average customer lifetime has most relevance to customer relationships created on a subscription basis (i.e., where the customer is active or not), such as the telecom industry, banking and insurance sectors, business-to-business cleaning services, and so on.

If the nature of the relationship is on a continuous basis, campaigns will tend to boost sales for a given period. In this case you should estimate the whale's body as the average extraordinary earnings per customer and for how long the campaign effect lasts. This topic is discussed in Chapter 5, since it deals with selling more to already existing customer groups.

If all the acquired customers have churned or the campaign effect has ceased, you can simply estimate the average length of the customer relations or the campaign effect and compare the effects of different campaigns using traditional hypothesis-driven statistics.

Based on the whale formula, you can now estimate the customer lifetime value per customer group acquired during the campaigns in the analysis (see Exhibit 4.3). If you subsequently combine the customer lifetime value results with historical knowledge about how many customers can be acquired per campaign dollar, you will have some very solid input about whether you can reach your objectives within your given campaign budget. You should also consider other things before you select campaigns, such as whether the campaign reaches out to customer groups within your strategic scope, whether there are more new customers to acquire in the given segments, and so on. Another alternative is to estimate the expected net present value of the future campaigns and subsequently the ROI; doing this means that from a business case perspective, you can evaluate whether to use your marketing budget on getting new customers or on the cross-selling and retention activities as presented in Chapters 5 and 6.

Finally you should also consider whether the costs of running the campaign will be reduced the second time around and therefore

Exhibit 4.3 Segment Prioritization Table

	Expected acquisition costs	Expected average value per year	Expected average lifetime in years	Expected customer lifetime value
Campaign 5	153	321	4,9	1420
Campaign 6	163	489	2,9	1255
Campaign 7	32	289	3,8	1066
Campaign 3	46	396	2,8	1063
Campaign 2	352	534	2,5	983
Campaign 4	264	296	3,9	890
Campaign 1	374	207	3,4	330

whether you need to correct your expected acquisition costs. There are many reasons why acquisition costs could be lower; for example, there would be reduced development costs on the second campaign. Another factor that might reduce your acquisition costs is that you can start making profiles of customers you acquired through your first campaign; for the second campaign, you can focus only on those customers with the highest propensity to buy and in this way increase the so-called hit rate. Also you can start targeting your offer and your market communication through the sales channels toward customers with the highest propensity to buy, which should increase the hit rate further. Doing this should decrease your acquisition cost per acquired customer even further, which is discussed in the next section.

PROFILING TARGET GROUPS

This section is aimed at acquisition processes owners who want to optimize already existing acquisition activities and have data about which customers were acquired during which campaigns. This section is not about identifying which campaigns are the most valuable ones but about improving the hit rate by understanding which customers have the highest propensity to buy and then redesigning the campaign

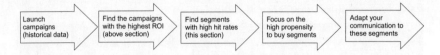

Exhibit 4.4 From First Launch to Profiled Launch of a Second Campaign

offer to these customer groups, as illustrated in Exhibit 4.4. This section therefore is closely linked to the last section since we describe how to improve your campaigns even more.

To complete this analysis, you must have data that can identify all the customers that you contacted during the campaign, which of these customers accepted your offer, and background information on all the customers that you targeted during the campaign. For example, this way of profiling could be used by organizations that make outbound sales calls to rent out vans to other businesses. The first step in such a campaign typically would be to get some contact information, which can be bought at a directory. These lists typically contain not only, say, 1,000 phone numbers or addresses but also background information about what industry the organizations are in, how many employees they have, turnover, whether it is a privately owned company, and so on. The next step for the organization is to contact all prospects on the list and register which prospects agreed to purchase the offer.

Then if the organization decides in the future to relaunch the same campaign, it has the option of profiling which customer segments have an increased propensity to buy using customer analytics. A CHAID algorithm (CHi square Automatic Interaction Detection) could be used for this sort of analysis; it belongs to the type of algorithms known as decision trees. Note that a decision tree can be based on many different algorithms with all sorts of exotic names.

A decision tree algorithm generates a treelike structured output, as presented in Exhibit 4.5. At the top node you can see that the overall hit rate of the whole campaign, or the sales rate, was 15% (150 customers from 1,000 calls). In this case the algorithm identifies "Industry" as a good way to find different hit rates; as we see, the hit rate for "Industry 2" has gone up to 35%. This means that if the company only had targeted that industry and called 1,000 customers within it, you would have gotten more than twice as many customers

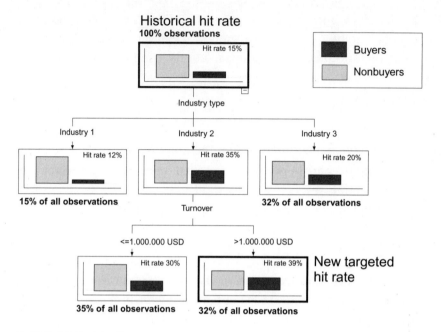

Exhibit 4.5 Decision Tree

out of the campaign (expected 350 rather than the 150). The algorithm also suggests that you should contact only those organizations with a turnover of more than $1,000, which brings the hit rate up to 39%.

The conclusion is that if you are about to do the same campaign again, you should only purchase prospects from the directory that are in "Industry 2" with a turnover of more than $1,000 in order to minimize your acquisition costs. It is important that you, as a company, also consider redesigning the offer in a way that will increase the customers' propensity to buy even more based on the target group characteristics.

WORKING WITH DECISION TREES

When you work with decision trees, some validation of the data is always needed in order to ensure that the patterns you identify in the data are generic for all customers within your scope, not just a local phenomenon in the data you analyze caused by sampling. The next list describes different ways you can validate your decision tree. Although some of the methods might seem very complex, they are standard functionalities in professional data mining tools. The first one, however, is the best one and known as common sense:

- Ask subject matter experts to make a sanity check on your model.
- Use other algorithms to find the same results.
- Split the data in two, and then see if the same results come out in both cases.
- Split the data in two, and then see whether the decision tree developed via the first half of the data could predict the buyers in the second half of the data.

For further information about data mining and how to validate data, see Chapter 4 of my previous book, *Business Analytics for Managers*, which provides a detailed discussion about the difference between data mining and statistics.[1]

Very often manually guiding the decision tree is also recommended, which means that it is the analyst, not the algorithm, who makes the split in the decision tree. You can discuss whether this is a relevant way of dividing the customers with subject matter experts as you are developing the decision tree. Perhaps you want to make the first split on turnover, since that is how your sales organization is built up—large account sales and small account sales—in order to align the results with the way that you are organized.

If you are in a market where your prospect list is, for instance, the top 100 companies in terms of size and you will call them all anyway, the decision tree method does not add a whole lot of value to your business apart from profiling where you have done best. This is because the essence of this method is to make you get more customers for your sales budget (reduce the acquisition costs via improved targeting). If your sales budget allows you to call all customers anyway, then there is no point in deselecting some prospects. There might be situations where you find that the costs of selling is higher that the customer lifetime value; then of course you should consider deselecting this customer group and voluntarily decreasing or reallocating your sales budget to other activities that also will reduce the overall acquisition costs per customer.

NEEDS-BASED SEGMENTATION CREATED FROM DATA WAREHOUSE DATA

If you used the decision tree presented in Exhibit 4.1, you have been guided to this section because you want to improve your acquisition campaigns and have no historical campaigning data. You have, however, indicated that you have access to data warehouse information or other kinds of transactional customer data. This transactional data could come from billing, sales, or customer relationship management (CRM) systems. Since we do not have campaign-specific data, we will rely on this data to guide us in a direction that gives us an improved understanding of the customer needs.

From an analytical perspective, we source customer data that describes customers' consumption patterns, we make a cluster analysis on this data, and interpret—supported by background variables— what needs have driven this customer behavior. Afterward it is up to the commercial decision makers to determine whether they can act on this segmentation or whether another segmentation model or approach has to be pursued. Exhibit 4.6 gives an overview of the process steps from an analytical perspective.

Cluster Analysis Based on Transactional Data

A car dealer once asked for a segmentation model for his local garage. He had a list of the last 350 cars he had sold in the previous year including what additional features had been sold with or came with the car. He also had a few records about the customers. From an analytical perspective, this means that we can generate a data set that

Exhibit 4.6 Methodological Flow of This Section

contains one line per sold car and one variable per car attribute (see Exhibit 4.7).

Based on cluster analysis (an algorithm that groups similar cases into segments and indicates how many homogeneous subgroups can be found in the data), a segmentation model based on four clusters was selected.

In general, cluster analysis can be done via a wide range of algorithms. The methodology used here was a hierarchical cluster analysis (you also read about this methodology in more detail in the section titled "Needs-Based Segmentation Created from Questionnaire Data" later in this chapter), which is an algorithm that first stacks cases into identical groups and then continues to stack the groups or individual cases into relatively similar groups until all the data is compiled into one big stack. The analyst who observes this process continuously evaluates whether the large stacks represent "logical" segments, from the perspective that the groups should be unique and can be interpreted as representing an actionable business need.

Validating the Cluster Solution

To confirm this four-group segmentation model, another kind of cluster algorithm was run on the same data with the aim of validating whether this grouping was a result of the individual algorithm used or a trend so general that it could also be picked up by other algorithms. The second algorithm was called a K-means cluster algorithm, which seeks to minimize the variance within a defined number of segments while at the same time maximizing the variance between the segments. This K-means algorithm came up with a similar segmentation model. Since this algorithm works in a very different way from cluster analysis, it is good for validation purposes. The K-means algorithm will not be explained in further detail in this book. However, it is standard functionality in most analytical software.

Understanding the Different Segments

The result of the cluster analysis is presented in Exhibit 4.8, where each of the four columns represents one of the four groups into which

Exhibit 4.7 Data Setup for Cluster Analysis

	Airbag driver seat	Airbag passenger seat	Airbag backseat	Baby chair	Add. music functionality	Chromed wheel caps	GPS navigation	Mobile phone additions	Turbo
1	1	1	1	1	1	1	1	0	1
2	1	1	0	1	0	1	1	1	1
3	0	1	1	1	1	1	0	1	0
4	1	0	1	1	1	1	1	0	0
5	0	1	1	1	1	0	1	1	0
6	1	1	1	0	0	1	1	0	0
7	0	0	1	1	0	1	0	0	0
8	1	1	1	0	1	1	1	1	1
9	1	0	1	1	1	0	1	1	1
10....	1	1	1	1	0	1	1	0	1

Exhibit 4.8 Result of the Cluster Analysis

	Percentage of customers buying that specific car feature			
	1. Everything	2. Fancy	3. Most things	4. Safety
Airbag driver seat	97%	60%	94%	95%
Airbag passenger seat	88%	50%	87%	94%
Airbag backseat	89%	40%	88%	90%
Baby chair	59%	2%	68%	62%
Add. music functionality	100%	95%	32%	30%
Chromed wheel caps	98%	94%	68%	38%
GPS navigation	88%	5%	80%	4%
Mobile phone additions	100%	58%	93%	80%
Turbo	88%	98%	55%	36%

all the sold cars were divided. From a data perspective, this means that we have added a new variable to the data set that describes to which of the four segments the particular case has been allocated. The rows in Exhibit 4.8 represent all the car features that were included in the cluster analysis. Based on this, 97% of the cars sold in segment 1, the "everything" segment, came with an airbag at the driver seat, 88% came with airbags at the passenger seats, and so on. The characteristic of the car sales, and therefore also the buyers behind these car sales, were:

- Segment 1 pretty much bought all the additional features.
- Segment 2 typically bought the more "fancy" features, such as additional music functionalities, special wheels, and a more powerful engine.
- Segment 3 bought nearly everything.
- Segment 4 bought the safety elements, such as air bags for all passengers and hands-free mobile phone equipment, which at

the time of the analysis was not standard equipment for all cars on the market.

After having identified and described the four buying patterns the next step was to add some background variables onto the segments. Since this will make it possible to identify which of the customers, coming through the door, belongs to which of the four segments, and how the salesperson should approach the different customers.

Identifying How to Target Relevant Segments

Exhibit 4.9 shows what sort of purchasers were behind the different car sales described by the four clusters (e.g., the car sales that made up the safety segment consisted of women or families). Based on this lead information, the car dealer implemented the model in his CRM system. When a new profile was entered, the customer was identified as possibly either "family" or "company" and based on this "family or company status," the prospect would receive an offer that reflected the buying profile:

- If it was a family person, the focus of all future communication sent would be on the safety aspects of the cars.
- If the person was a woman in search of or buying a car for herself, the communication would focus on safety and the freedom of selecting "only the extras that you want."

Exhibit 4.9 Features versus Background Information

		Buyers' profile			
		Family	Female	Male	Company
Clusters	1. Everything	29	19	24	16
	2. Fancy	26	7	43	0
	3. Most	2	19	20	25
	4. Safety	65	40	12	3
Total		122	85	99	29

- If the person was a male in search of or buying a car for himself, the promotion would focus on the fancy elements that a car can be delivered with and the freedom of selecting "only the extras that you want."

- If it was a company, the promotion would focus on the fact that this car had the full package and the company should only worry about "whether a turbo should be included or not!"

The physical surroundings of the car dealer were also changed so that the cars were presented in four clusters so salespeople could take customers directly to the most relevant area. A little playground was also set up in the family area, golf equipment was displayed in the male area, and green plants were set out in the female area. The company area included a desk with different brochures about company financing and tax rules.

Other Examples

Similar cluster analysis has been run on software customers who had a modular buying pattern (e.g., do you want the software package to include data mining algorithms, graphical modules, advanced statistics, Web publishing functionality, etc.?). Based on the same analytical procedure, segments were identified, clear links to appropriate industries were established, and offers were designed to fit these links. Leads/lists of prospects within the relevant industries were bought afterward and campaigning was initiated.

The same methodology was also used in the telecom industry where, based on billing information, we could see which features customers used (e.g., multimedia messaging, text messaging, foreign calls, financial limits, voice mail, etc.). Based on these consumption features, we developed a segmentation model and identified which individual stores typically acquired each of the segments. Armed with this knowledge, we could go back into these stores and present our telecom products according to local customer needs. Some stores would focus on "ease of calling your family living abroad" paired with a telecom product that gave discounts for customers who talk a lot to destinations outside the country. In other stores with many young people and their families, they would focus on promoting text-messaging products to the younger people and target information about credit limits to the parent who would be the legal contract holder until the teen turned 18 years old.

VALUE-BASED SEGMENTATION CREATED FROM DATA WAREHOUSE INFORMATION

This section is about how, based on typical DW information, you can identify the most valuable customers. Usually it is recommended that you start your activities by understanding what your customers want, since this is the essence of being able to create an effective sales process. However, there can be many reasons why you cannot establish a needs-based segmentation. Perhaps your organization did not provide you with proper guidance about which segments to pursue. Perhaps the data does not show any different needs among your customers, or there simply are no different customer needs. Perhaps you only want to target one of the segments within the needs-based segmentation model and from now on you want to approach your prospects based on who historically generates the highest profits. However, since we do not have any campaign data to go by, which is a prior assumption of this section, we can look into our DW and profile the most valuable customers and target them. In many ways this exercise is very similar to what is presented in the section called "Profiling Target Groups." Focus is not on improving the hit rate of an existing campaign but on how to identify valuable customers for a new campaign.

Overall, this method is very valuable in situations where the list of potential customers is too long for you to contact them all. In such a situation, you would prefer to have this list sorted somehow, so that you can target your sales efforts toward customers with the highest return on sales investment first.

Setting Up the Data

From a customer intelligence perspective, a value-based approach to segmentation can be achieved by setting up a data mart with one line per customer, including the customer lifetime value and the appropriate variables regarding how you can identify your leads. If you cannot estimate the customer lifetime value (measured in $1,000 in Exhibit 4.10), you can use a variable describing the turnover, yield per customer, or however else you wish to define a valuable customer. To read more about how to calculate the lifetime value per customer, see the section "Finding the Most Valuable Target Group" in this chapter. From an analytical perspective, this is a relatively simple task since the needed variables typically can be found in the DW and simply extracted into the analytical base mart with one line per customer and all the relevant attributes as columns (see Exhibit 4.10).

Exhibit 4.10 Analytical Base Table for a Value-Based Segmentation Approach

	CLV	Income	Gender	Age	Education years	Job type	Nationality	Education level
1	87	4500	Female	23,00	12	No Job	National	High school
2	86	4800	Female	23,25	12	No Job	National	High school
3	116	4980	Female	23,25	8	No Job	National	Primary school
4	92	4920	Female	23,33	12	Blue collar	National	High school
5	91	4500	Female	23,42	12	No Job	National	High school
6	82	4500	Female	23,42	12	No Job	National	High school
7	91	4500	Female	23,42	12	No Job	National	High school
8	82	4500	Female	23,58	12	No Job	National	High school
9	122	4980	Female	23,67	12	No Job	National	High school
10	91	4500	Female	23,67	12	No Job	National	High school
11	83	4500	Female	23,67	12	No Job	National	High school

	CLV	Income	Gender	Age	Education years	Job type	Nationality	Education level
12	83	4500	Female	23,75	12	No Job	National	High school
13	85	4500	Female	24,00	12	No Job	Immigrant	High school
14	104	4620	Female	24,00	12	No Job	National	High school
15	98	4980	Female	24,08	12	No Job	National	High school
16	92	4500	Female	24,08	12	No Job	National	High school
17	111	4490	Female	24,17	12	Blue collar	National	High school
18	112	4980	Female	24,17	12	No Job	National	High school
19	89	4500	Female	24,33	12	No Job	National	High school
20	94	4500	Female	24,33	12	No Job	National	High school
21	90	4380	Female	24,33	8	No Job	National	Primary school
22	138	4860	Female	24,33	12	No Job	National	High school
23	98	4800	Female	24,33	12	No Job	National	High school
24	111	4620	Male	24,42	12	Blue collar	Immigrant	High school
25	95	5100	Female	24,42	12	No Job	National	High school
26	79	4500	Female	24,50	12	No Job	National	High school
27	92	4380	Female	24,50	12	No Job	National	High school
28	107	4620	Female	24,58	12	No Job	National	High school
29	102	4800	Female	24,58	12	No Job	National	High school
30	85	4500	Female	24,67	12	No Job	National	High school
31	99	4380	Female	24,67	12	No Job	National	High school
32	102	4560	Male	24,75	12	No Job	Immigrant	High school

Analyzing the Data

When the data is set up in this way, you can use pivot table cubes to slice and dice your way down through the dimension until you find the relevant segments. Alternatively you can use decision tree technology, which allows you to use algorithms as guidance on how to do the best splits and work interactively with results. Decision trees are presented in great detail in the section "Profiling Target Groups."

How to Use the Results

The finding of this decision tree in Exhibit 4.11 is that of the 474 cases that went into the analysis, we can identify 52 that are significantly more valuable from a customer lifetime value perspective. Hence you could choose to target specialist, trainees, white collars, and technicians with an income of more than $10,992 per month for your next campaign.

When you have found your most valuable segments, this insight will also very often feed back into the market communication that

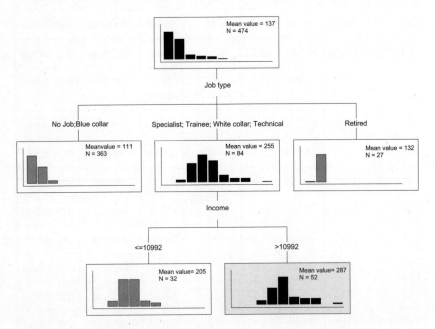

Exhibit 4.11 Decision Tree Approach to Identifying Most Valuable Segments

you use, since you now will have increased knowledge about which segments you target and can calibrate what you offer and how you offer it to the target group. Alternatively you might find that you can at relatively small cost target the campaign to fit the individual segments, in which case you end up with more campaigns in terms of whom to target, what to offer, and how to get the message through (channels). At the end of the section "Needs-Based Segmentation Created from Data Warehouse Data," you can find a few examples that can serve as inspiration.

NEEDS-BASED SEGMENTATION CREATED FROM QUESTIONNAIRE DATA

This section takes you through how you can make a needs-based segmentation on already existing questionnaire data. This segmentation can be used to identify target groups for individual one-off campaigns; alternatively this segmentation can be used as a first step toward scoring your entire customer base in your DW according to the same principles. (You can read more about this in Chapter 1 in the section called "Segmentation and Data Warehousing.")

The process presented in this chapter (see Exhibit 4.12) includes five steps. It is quite long but also typical for how, once in awhile, you have to simplify questionnaire data in order to allow analysts to make some overarching conclusions; rather than present a long series of interesting but unactionable correlations.

In the next example, all that the travel agent sold was skiing trips. There was only one product but many destinations, and they could be looked up in a catalog. The company's first step was to hire two students to make a survey identifying the different customer groups and their needs.

Exhibit 4.12 Content and Order of This Section

Identify Usable Questionnaire Data

When I became involved in the analysis, the two students had made the survey but were drowning in data. They had gotten into this situation because they were uncertain about what to ask for, so they had simply asked for too much data and still did not know where to start. The first step was simply to keep all the questions that, in one way or the other, measured an attitude toward all the different elements in winter sport traveling. The rest was laid aside in this first phase (see Exhibit 4.13).

Reduce Attributes to Create Simple and Useful Data

The next step was to run a principal component analysis (PCA is also known as an exploratory factor analysis) on the data. The purpose of using the PCA was to reduce a long list of attributes (the many variables going into the analysis) into a smaller number of factors (the few new variables being created and appended to the data set by the analysis). In this particular case we needed to do data reduction since 37 attributes with overlapping content had to be reduced to a more manageable level. For example, "How important is it for you that you can go out at night on a pub crawl?" and "Would you like to do after-ski partying at night?" are overlapping in their content since they basically are asking the customers about the same need.

A PCA groups the highly correlated questions in a survey. This is because the questions typically correlate for the very simple reason that they ask about the same thing; hence if you would agree that you are "interested in pub crawling," you probably also would "like to do partying at night" if you are a party animal. From a statistical point of view we say that the two questions share information simply because they measure the same thing. The output of a PCA is knowledge about how many groups of questions correlate in your data set and which questions belong to which groups. Should you find that all your attributes correlate into three groups, you have what is known as three latent factors (i.e., even though you might be asking ten different questions, the customers only care about three things, perhaps price, speed of delivery, and the kindness of your staff). In this way you are going from describing your customer via ten variables to only doing it via three new ones generated as an output of the analysis. It

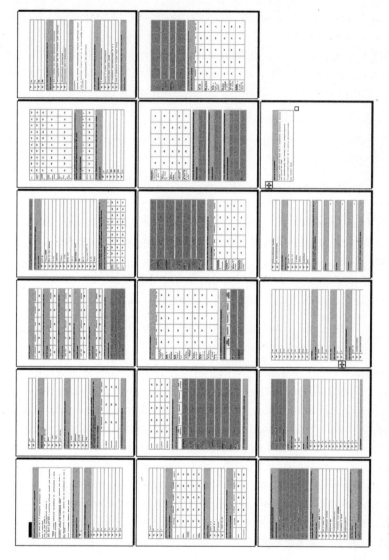

Exhibit 4.13 Only the Dark Gray Elements of the Questionnaire Were Kept

91

is a bit like making a cluster analysis, grouping the variables rather than the observations.

We found that the questions fell into seven groups. Based on what the attributes had in common, we concluded that the combination of seven things that skiers evaluate their skiing trips by were:

1. Ability to do after-ski partying
2. Whether people like the ski guide in terms of knowledge and personal maturity
3. The facilities of the area in terms of ski lifts, shops, charming city, toilets, centrally placed, etc.
4. The participation and support of the guide when showing slopes, renting skis, information meetings, parties, etc.
5. Other activities such as dinner arrangements, wellness, quiet surroundings, and ski schools at the location
6. Whether people can cook themselves or can use restaurants
7. Whether there would be someone to help them in case of accidents or problems with housing

Thus, instead of having 37 questions to analyze, we were now down to seven factors. This meant that instead of analyzing 37 variables, we could now focus on the seven created as new variables in the data mart. This would give us a good overview about what is important for skiers and thus simplify the picture. However, it is also important to make sure that the dimensions included in the cluster analysis are unique. If you have five questions that basically retrieve the same information from the respondents, those questions will tend to dominate the cluster analysis at the expense of equally important latent factors that are represented with relatively few questions. Since you can set the output factors of a PCA to have a correlation of zero, this is the same as saying that these seven dimensions all are unique. We would avoid having that many variables about the same subject, because they would skew the cluster analysis. The costs of doing a PCA going from 37 input dimensions to seven is that you throw away a lot of information—in this case 51%. However, segmentation is all about simplifying the truth, which is necessary if you cannot treat your customers on a one-to-one basis, so the discarding of information is not alarming.

Cluster Analysis to Make Homogeneous Groups

The next step was to make a hierarchical cluster analysis, which works by the principle that if two cases (questionnaire respondents) score exactly the same, they will be grouped first. When all the "clones" are grouped, then one by one the groups of clones or the cases with no clones are grouped based on how similar they are. This will go on until all groups are merged into one. As an analyst, you will stop this merging process at a point where the "big" groups are merged, since a big group could represent a segment. The stopping point in this particular analysis was when there were 31 groups left (see Exhibit 4.14). The four large groups were kept as they were, and the last observations were merged into a last segment. (You can read about how to make cluster analyses in the section titled "Needs-Based Segmentation Based Created from Warehouse Data" in this chapter.)

	Cluster no.	No. of clusters							
		34	33	32	31	30	29	28	27
Counts of cases within each group at the given step	1	457	457	457	457	629	629	629	716
	2	42	42	42	42	42	42	42	42
	3	2	2	2	2	2	29	29	29
	4	123	172	172	172	4	4	4	4
	5	4	4	4	4	87	87	87	138
	6	87	87	87	87	117	117	138	5
	7	117	117	117	117	5	5	5	1
	8	5	5	5	5	1	1	1	4
	9	1	1	1	1	4	4	4	10
	10	4	4	4	4	21	21	10	4
	11	21	21	21	21	10	10	4	11
	12	10	10	10	10	4	4	11	12
	13	49	4	4	4	11	11	12	8
	14	4	11	11	11	12	12	8	9
	15	11	11	11	12	8	8	9	2
	16	11	8	8	8	9	9	2	4
	17	8	9	9	9	2	2	4	4
	18	9	2	2	2	27	4	4	5
	19	2	27	27	27	4	4	5	3
	20	27	1	1	4	4	5	3	3
	21	1	4	4	4	5	3	3	1
	22	4	4	4	5	3	3	1	3
	23	4	5	5	3	3	1	3	1
	24	5	3	3	3	1	3	1	1
	25	3	3	3	1	3	1	1	3
	26	3	1	1	3	1	1	3	1
	27	1	1	3	1	1	3	1	1
	28	1	1	1	1	3	1	1	
	29	1	1	1	3	1	1		
	30	1	3	3	1	1			
	31	3	2	1	1				
	32	2	1	1					
	33	1	1						
	34	1							

Exhibit 4.14 Cluster Selection Point

Exhibit 4.15 Finding the Needs of the Clusters by Finding the Average Factor Scores per Segment

Cluster and number of respondent	After-ski	Guides in general	Facilities	Participation of the guide	Ability to relax	Food included	Handling of difficult situations
1 (457)	.42	.04	−.15	−.15	−.38	.05	.23
2 (172)	−.81	.49	.26	.39	−.01	.77	.01
3 (87)	−.45	.00	.68	.45	−.40	−1.33	.11
4 (117)	.33	.16	−.12	.46	1.51	−.32	.28
5 (192)	−.26	−.62	−.11	−.48	.17	−.02	−.78

Now we can learn about the needs of these five segments by estimating the average score on the seven factors generated from the PCA, which also is set to an average of zero and a standard deviation of 1 (see Exhibit 4.15).

Based on the average score of the five segments on the seven factors, we could now start interpreting what their needs were:

1. Cluster 1 was called "Wine and safety" since it only scored high on after-skiing and support when problems. (This was the largest group and included 457 of the respondents.)

2. Cluster 2 was interested in adult guides and the inclusion of food, and less interested in after-skiing.

3. Cluster 3 was interested in the facilities at the resort and less on the food.

4. Cluster 4 was more interested in the nonskiing facilities that allowed you to relax.

5. Cluster 5, consisting of the last small groups, had a tendency to be less interested in the services provided by the guide.

Using Background Information to Profile the Segments

To validate this segmentation model, we analyzed the results by cross-tabbing the segments and other input variables from the ques-

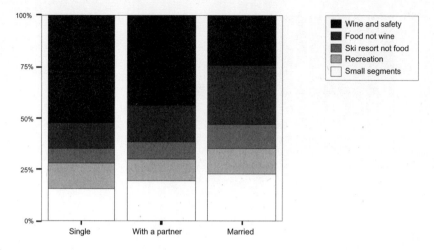

Exhibit 4.16 Verifying the Clusters

tionnaire that until now had been deselected in the analysis (see Exhibit 4.16).

All these cross-tabs confirmed that it was reasonable to believe we had a robust model. We could rely on this robustness because we learned that singles were often the most interested in partying whereas married couples typically were more interested in the food. This is, in itself, not a final proof, but it is a clear indication that our model describes the same reality as the one experienced skiers presented to us.

Identifying How to Target Selected Segments

Based on Exhibit 4.17, we learned that potential customers (with no previous ski travel) were interested in the alternative activities since they realized that they might not be interested in skiing constantly throughout their stay; the more ski trips a person had made, the more interest he or she had in the ski resort and less on restaurants. Therefore, sales agents were instructed to uncover first whether the customers, or anyone in the party they represented, were first-time travelers. Based on this analysis, the holiday vendor would promote alternative activities to any first-time travelers. If the customers were experienced skiers, the vendor would determine what segment they

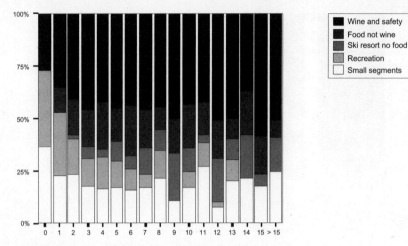

Number of times the respondent has been on skiing holiday before

Exhibit 4.17 Using the Model

were in: If they fit the "Wine and safety" segment, the vendor would promote the late-night activities; in the "Food not wine" segment, the vendor would promote the early-evening activities; in the "Ski resort no food" segment, the vendor would promote the daily activities (e.g., slopes and lifts, etc.)

DESIGNING A QUESTIONNAIRE

Analysts and project managers with no useful DW or historical questionnaire data to make segmentation from will have to make a survey themselves, if they still want to make a data-driven segmentation model. This section briefly explains how you can design a questionnaire. If you follow the general guidelines of this section, the resulting data will be structured in the same way as the data in the section "Needs-Based Segmentation Created from Questionnaire Data," which means that you also can use the same analytical approach.

There are many good reasons for using a questionnaire to identify the needs of your customers. (This was discussed in more detail in Chapter 1 in the "Segmentation and Data Warehousing" section.) In brief, however, what you get from a DW is transactional customer behavior recorded at some touch points, but what you want to know are the customer needs that drive this behavior. Simply put, customer

Transactional customer data — the data reflecting what your information systems capture	***BI***
Customer behavior — what the customer did	⇕
Customer needs — what the customer perceives your company to be able to enable	***Marketing***

Exhibit 4.18 From Data to Customer Needs

behavior could be to buy an electric drill machine, but what the customer really wants could be to make a nice sitting room with pictures on the walls. Therefore, you may want to consider asking the customers themselves what they want rather than focusing only on their behavior (see Exhibit 4.18).

The benefit of a questionnaire is that you can ask customers specifically about their needs and what drives their behavior. If you work with DW data, you will try to map customer behavior and try to understand what needs generated the behavior based on the data. Since the overall purpose of segmentation is to understand customer needs, the use of questionnaire data can provide a segmentation model with fewer assumptions. On the negative side, typically high costs are associated with making surveys, it will take longer before you have your data, and you will get data only from those customers who choose to respond to your survey or interview. The right choice depends on your situation; if possible, you should use both DW and survey data for your analysis. If you are starting a marketing function in a product-oriented organization that historically has not gathered data about customer needs, a needs-based study might be the right thing to do, no matter how good your DW information is because you simply need to understand the basics of the industry that you are about to do marketing in.

If you choose to go for the questionnaire approach, the best single piece of advice is: Start by deciding what you want to learn, not with the questionnaire itself. Often beginners start by drafting a lot of questions that they think are relevant. After they have made a long, extensive list, they send out the survey with the hope that during the analysis phase, they will come up with the needed answers. Sometimes they will and sometimes they will not; it really is up to luck and intuition, as this quotation indicates: "If you do not know where you are going, you will risk ending up somewhere else." In other words, you may end up with a data set that allows for a lot of conclusions but not necessarily the right ones.

There are eight steps involved in making a questionnaire:

1. **Know what you are trying to achieve.** Customer analytics of this sort is about generating decision support, so you must understand exactly what decision you or your stakeholders want to make and how can you support this decision with relevant knowledge or information. In general, stop thinking about this as a "study" and identify what specific business processes you can change based on the conclusions of the survey.

2. **Consider how the data should be presented in order for you to make the necessary decisions.** Do you want to see a segmentation model, will averages and simple statistics do in a table format, should some business case be developed, and so on?

3. **Know which statistical methodology to use.** When you know how the data should be presented in order for you to make the decision, you should have a very good idea about the methodology required. Must you do PCA, hypothesis testing, cluster analysis, or tables before you can present the data and make your decisions?

4. **Know how the input data should look.** This is based on which statistical method you use. Can you use yes-or-no answers, should it be satisfaction scores from 1 to 7, can you use open text fields, or would you ask the respondents in units like minutes, volumes purchased per months, or specific prices?

5. **Start creating the questions for the questionnaire.** Make sure that they generate the right data for the chosen statistical method and give the right decision support in a format desired by the decision maker.

6. **Consider who should respond to the survey, how many respondents you will need for your analysis, and how many responses it is realistic for you to get.** Based on what you find here, you might want to reconsider points 1 to 5. again or possibly start to incentivize the respondents to improve response rates. Also it is essential to consider whether this

survey is something that you want to do only once. If you want to repeat it later, how will you reward respondents and store their contact information?

7. **Consider whether to include other elements in the questionnaire,** such as variables that will make it easier to compare the responses from this survey with all the customers in your DW, if at a later stage you will make a score back to your DW as discussed in Chapter 1 in the section called "Segmentation and Data Warehousing."

8. **Make sure that the questionnaire is crisp and condensed, supported by relevant communication that you send to your customers.** At the end of the day, the questionnaire is also communication that will effect customer perceptions and feelings about you as a company.

Next we list a basic framework for how to make a questionnaire that can give you input about customer needs and your competitive situation. These three questions should be repeated for every relevant customer need (e.g., need for a quiet vacuum cleaner) or product attribute (e.g., noise reduction bottom).

1. How important is the design of a vacuum cleaner to you? ("Unimportant" to "Very important" on a 1 to 5 or 7 scale. Always give respondents the option of answering "Don't know.")

2. How well designed are our vacuum cleaners? ("Not well designed" to "Very well designed", on a 1 to 5 or 7 scale, etc.)

3. How well is our "Best in class" vacuum cleaner design among competitors?

If you choose this way of designing your questionnaire, you will also be able to generate some competitive decision support, which in itself might be very valuable for your organization, simply testing whether your company scores significant lower than the best in class provider as presented in Exhibit 4.19. The same data set can also be used to make a needs-based segmentation model through the use of PCA and cluster analysis, as mentioned earlier, using subject matter

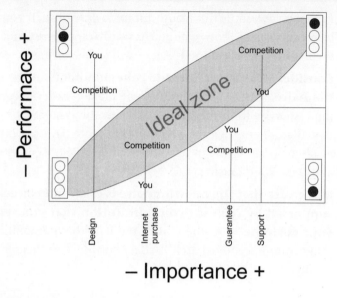

Exhibit 4.19 Performance Importance Plot

expert interviews for input, as presented in the next section. For the rest of this section, we focus on how to make a competitive evaluation from this survey concept.

Exhibit 4.19 provides input on what is important to the respondents and whether you are perceived as a provider of it. Perhaps you find elements in which you are perceived to be the market leader, and that are important to your customers. You can use these as themes for future marketing campaigns. From a strategic perspective, doing this would be equal to using your internal strengths to exploit market opportunities. Alternatively, you might identify weaknesses that you should report to your product development or strategy department.

To illustrate the difference between the four quadrants in Exhibit 4.19, some traffic lights have been included. If you find elements placed in the red light zone, you are not capable of delivering on some of the most important customer needs or attributes. Give these areas first priority, particularly if the competition is beating you on these elements. The top right corner is the green zone, which describes the elements that are important to customers and that your company delivers well. The yellow zone represents those elements that your company delivers well but that are not so important to customers. This also raises these questions: Are you as a company spending too many resources on delivering on less relevant yellow elements? Would you be better off reallocating some of these resources elsewhere? Also consider whether to develop the individual elements, accept their position, or instead of changing what you offer, change to whom you offer it.

SEGMENTATION BASED ON WORKSHOPS

Consulting subject matter experts is often the quickest way to segment customers and probably an exercise that you will have to do anyway in order for you to validate your segmentation model and to create stakeholder buy-in. After all, you have to keep in mind that statistics usually provide only some signals about reality; the real world has to explain itself in order for your conclusion to be more than speculation.

A logistics provider in the business-to-business industry can construct needs-based segmentation by inviting some key account managers to a workshop where the provider asks the subject matter experts to name the different customer types with different logistical needs. Customer types do not have to be defined by industries; different customer needs also are generated as a result of their individual positions within industries. Some will compete on price, others on quality and differentiation; some might be producers while others simply trade in these commodities, and so on. In this example we will only define the different customer needs based on their industry.

The first step in this process is to have the subject matter experts name two different industries and list what makes the industries different. These two customer types could be clothing stores and factories doing machinery production. Here key account managers might agree that they differ since it is extremely important for machinery production customers to have their cargo at the factories at the expected time to prevent the production process from coming to a standstill. When clothing is trucked, however, its date of arrival is not that critical; the cargo can be a day or two late without causing too many problems. Another difference between the two industries could be that, to a

Exhibit 4.20 Two Groups and Two Needs (Scores Range from 1 to 5, where 5 Is Very Important)

	Delivery on time	People service
Clothing	3	3
Machinery production	5	1

Exhibit 4.21 Three Groups and Four Needs (Scores Range from 1 to 5, where 5 Is Very Important)

	Delivery on time	People service	Price driven	Relation
Clothing	3	3	2	3
Machinery production	5	1	3	5
DIY	1	3	5	2

larger degree, clothing stores ask the logistics provider for advice when making complex transports; machinery production facilities typically have their own logistics department and huge transportation experience. These findings are summarized in Exhibit 4.20.

The next segment that might come into the minds of key account managers could be deliveries to do-it-yourself (DIY) shops, which are well known for their focus on the transportation costs and which, however, can accept a late delivery. This new information is also included on the table along with the fact that production plants in general are more interested in entering long-term contracts, which might be something that comes to mind since DIY customers are extremely transactional in their behavior. This is all summarized in Exhibit 4.21.

When the exercise is over, a matrix as in Exhibit 4.22 might result. Other customer groups might be included, such as "New customers" with focus on customer service until they can use the Internet booking facilities themselves, or "Large branded customers" who perhaps typically would use many logistics providers and often ask for a quick price in order to pick the cheapest partner.

The next exercise is to calibrate the scores of the needs in case the scores across all the customer groups are very similar. Either you

Exhibit 4.22 Seven Groups and Six Needs (Scores Range from 1 to 5, where 5 Is Very Important)

	Delivery on time	People service	Price driven	Relation	Flexibility in delivery	Special equipment
Clothing	3	3	2	3	2	3
Machinery production	5	1	3	5	4	1
DIY	1	3	5	2	1	1
Supermarkets	5	5	3	3	5	1
Food	5	4	4	3	5	5
Chemical production	4	1	2	4	4	3
IT	2	3	2	5	5	1

should score the groups differently so real differences are shown, or you should remove the need if it does not hold any basis for differentiation between the customer groups anyway. In Exhibit 4.22, we might, for example, consider why no customer groups scored 1 on the need for cheap logistics and long-term relationships with the trucker.

The final two exercises are about reducing the number of needs if some describe the same thing, and reducing the number of customer groups if some have the same needs. This exercise typically can be done simply by taking a very good look at the numbers; alternatively, you can use a dendrogram, which is produced as output when making a hierarchical cluster analysis. A dendrogram is a graphical presentation of which groups are the most similar and therefore are grouped together at an early stage by the algorithm when doing a cluster analysis. You can read more about hierarchical cluster analysis in the section "Needs-Based Segmentation Created from Warehouse Data." The dendrogram shows that "relational need" and "flexibility need" are combined very early, indicated with the shadow in Exhibit 4.23.

This first analysis, aimed at combining very similar customer needs, indicates that the customers that are very relational in their

Dendrogram using average linkage (between groups)

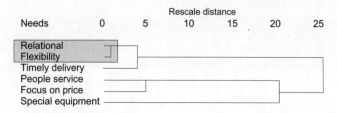

Exhibit 4.23 Dendrogram Indicating Groups of Similar Customer Needs

Dendrogram using average linkage (between groups)

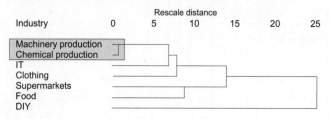

Exhibit 4.24 Dendrogram Indicating Similar Customer Groups

approach to the logistics provider (as opposed to transactional price hunters) also are the ones that require the most flexibility from the logistics provider. If we look into which industries score high on these two needs, it is the production industries and the information technology vendors. From a logistics perspective, this need could mean that the logistics company is seen as an integrated part of the customers' internal supply chains, which is why these industries are willing to invest in partnerships via long-term contracts. If we believe that, we can collapse the two needs into one overarching group called the "need for stable internal processes." Timely delivery could potentially also be included in the grouping.

When or if the two needs are combined, we are finally ready for the last step in the segmentation process: to see if we have groups of customers with similar needs. (From a statistical perspective, you cluster the cases rather than the variables, as we did in Exhibit 4.23.)

Exhibit 4.24 suggests that we could consider merging the two customer groups that both work with production facilities since they in general are interpreted to have the same logistics needs. Whether to do this or not is a business decision.

By using subject matter experts' statistics, you have created a segmentation model. As a next step, you could validate it via a survey to your customers. If the survey confirms the segmentation model, you might also be able to identify which customers in your customer base belong to which segment on an individual basis; doing this will enable you to report on turnover, earnings, and churn per segment. Chapter 7 discusses how to work with this lag information.

SEEING THE ACQUISITION PROCESS FROM A DYNAMIC PERSPECTIVE

This chapter is about how to use lead information for acquisition processes and is structured according to how your organization is set up to perform these processes, as illustrated in Exhibit 4.25. Based on what data you have available, customer analytics will, to a varying extent, be able to create value for your organization. It is therefore important to recognize that you must invest in data before you can harvest the benefits from customer analytics. Whether you should invest in customer analytics as a starting point or not is essentially a strategic question for your organization. You can look into your organizational or marketing strategy and identify whether customer

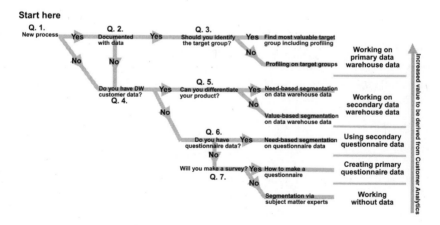

Exhibit 4.25 Improving Your Lead Information for Acquisition Processes

analytics can make your organization meet its strategic objectives. If you find that customer analytics can enable your organization to meet its strategic objectives, you can investigate where in Exhibit 4.25 from a strategic perspective you should be and where you are. Based on the discrepancies you find, you will also get a clear indication about what challenges lie ahead of you.

Chapter 8 provides some tools that enable you to analyze the current maturity level of your organization when it comes to customer analytics from an overall CRM/marketing process perspective.

NOTE

1. Laursen, Gert, Thorlund, Jesper. *Business Analytics for Managers: Taking Business Intelligence beyond Reporting*, (Hoboken, NJ: John Wiley & Sons, 2010).

CHAPTER 5

Lead Information: What You Need to Know before Launching New Sales Activities

If I could optimize your sales by telling you which customers you should sell what to and when—would that be of any interest to you?

This chapter is about how you can use customer analytics to improve your sales processes to your existing customer base. Since this can be done in many ways depending on the maturity of your information systems, the beginning of this chapter leads you toward a section that might serve as inspiration for you, taking your current situation into account. Each of these sections then focuses on the relationship among data, analytical methodology, and how you can integrate the results into the way that you do business. If you would like to read more about change management, stakeholder management, conflict resolution, and so on, read the first half of Chapter 3 as inspiration.

Either you are reading this book from one end to the other or you are reading this chapter because Chapter 2 recommended that you do so. This chapter focuses on how customer analytics can support your organization in getting new customers. Strategic reasons for focusing on acquisition processes may include:

- Your objectives clearly indicate that your success is directly linked to your ability to acquire new customers.
- You are placed in sales with no responsibility for what happens after the contract is closed.
- You are strategically positioned in a market with a relatively low penetration compared to expected market potential.
- You have a relatively small customer base according to your strategic ambitions.
- You are introducing new products to the market and they are not well received by your existing customer base.
- Your company is pursuing growth via market differentiation (entering new markets).

There might be other reasons for embarking on cross- and up-selling initiatives, since this simply might be something companies have to do on a continuous basis. You might also have been given this focus as a result of your company strategy, where increasing volumes per customer is a specified tactical maneuver. Alternatively, it could be your own decision or one coming from within your department as a functional strategy that you must be able to execute successfully in order to meet some strategic objectives. Under all circumstances, you are now in a situation where you need to know how well customer analytics can give you guidance about which customers to sell what to and when.

This chapter is about how you work with and generate *lead* information *before* creating a new sales campaign focused on your existing customer base. The concept of lead information was described in Chapter 1. In brief, however, lead information describes the type of information that you as a commercial department require in order to create new or take your existing sales processes to the next level.

You should also read Chapter 7, which focuses on how to create and work with *lag* information (lag information is distinct in the sense that it is used to monitor and optimize within the framework of an existing process). Lag information is therefore something you work with *while running* the campaigns. Finally you should also read Chapter 8, which is about *learning* information. This will tell you how to use customer analytics systematically for organizational learning *after running* a campaign.

BEFORE YOUR CAMPAIGN

This section describes a series of analytical options you have, based on assumptions closely linked to your objectives and the maturity of your organization. In general, customer analytics is heavily associated with business intelligence and usage of data warehouse (DW) data, particularly when it comes to selling to an already existing customer base. In this chapter we also discuss the use of subject matter experts and questionnaires as data sources, because *customer intelligence should not be defined by where the data comes from but by the type of decision support that it enables.* (See Chapter 1 for a more detailed discussion.) This chapter therefore promotes different analytical methodologies that can be used depending on the information you have available in your organization. The chapter also promotes a path of how to become information driven in the future.

You can either read the full chapter for inspiration, or you can go to the parts of the chapter that you find the most relevant. Exhibit 5.1 can show you where to go, if you choose to go directly to a specific section. Start using the decision tree in the upper left corner. Based on your response to the five questions, you will get direction about what is likely to be relevant for you. The five questions are:

1. **Is it an existing business process?** The purpose of this question is to uncover whether this campaign is something you have done before. If this is a completely new process, there cannot be any historical data to support your analytical efforts. If it is a known process, you might have a lot of performance data to learn from.

Start here

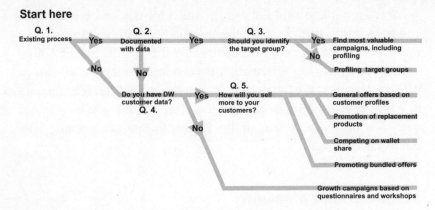

Exhibit 5.1 Chapter Structure

2. **If this is not a new process, does data exist about the process?** If the answer is no, from a customer intelligence perspective you are as well off as if you had to establish this process for the first time. If the answer is yes, there might exist some usable lag information describing historical performance of the campaigns that can be worked with analytically and turned into lead information.

3. **Should you identify target groups?** This question looks at whether it is a part of the assignment to pick the most valuable campaign among a series of alternative campaigns or whether it is a given campaign/acquisition process that you wish to optimize. Two analytical methodologies that support each other well, since when you have picked the most attractive campaign you still have the option of optimizing it even more.

4. **Do you have access to DW data?** Even though we do not have any historical data on the specific sales process that you want to work with, we could still be interested in using DW information if it is available.

5. **How will you sell more to your customers?**

   ■ By promoting **general offers** depending on their customer characteristics (e.g., designing and promoting offers based on customer profiles).

- By promoting **future offers**, also known as replacement products (e.g., you typically only have one car at a time, so which type should be your next one?).

- By competing on **wallet share** (e.g., if a customer potentially can have multiple subcontractors, how can you compete on analytics?).

- By promoting **bundled offers** (e.g., designing offers and promotions based on what people typically purchase together).

FINDING THE MOST VALUABLE CAMPAIGNS

This section was written for process owners who want to optimize their existing sales activities directed to their existing customer base and who have DW information about which customers buy what as a result of which campaign. The aim of this section is to show how you can identify which campaigns are the most valuable for your company from a return on investment (ROI) perspective. At the same time this analysis also uncovers which campaigns give the lowest return and potentially should be stopped since they simply might represent a waste of resources. This way of working with performance data is also known as marketing automation. If this is a new term for you, you can read more about it in Chapter 8.

The purpose of this section is to create a framework that allows you to identify which campaigns within all your cross-selling activities perform well. Apart from telling you which campaigns you should keep active, you will also learn how to identify the common denominator of all successful campaigns. This analysis therefore will help you understand from an overall perspective the characteristics of a successful campaign and potentially will improve the way you design campaigns in the future. A typical example is how you can produce lead information from lag information. You should keep the saying among controllers in mind: "It is likely that the most valuable person in this organization is an innovative person who continuously challenges the way we do campaigns. There is, however, no doubt either that the second most valuable person is the controller who stops all of the innovative person's activities that are about to fail." Also keep in mind that some individuals are extremely good at presenting and promoting their ideas to stakeholders, and there are also some who are good at creating profitable campaigns. Since these two kinds of people are not always the same, continuously monitor and learn who delivers quality in your organization.

If you follow the approach of this section, you will learn to select a series of campaigns or selling activities that you will want to keep active. The next section shows you how to optimize existing campaigns.

In Chapter 4, we explained how to find the most valuable target groups when it comes to acquisition processes. This was done by estimating the expected customer lifetime value using various forms of statistics. This way of measuring the effect of your marketing and sales initiatives on a campaign level is usually too imprecise for campaign evaluation since the customer's acceptance of an offer is a smaller phenomenon that has only a minor effect on the full customer lifetime journey. Therefore, you should focus on when the campaign has an effect and when the effect wears off again and use the time-limited effect only as an input to the business case that evaluates your campaign performance. There are of course times where a campaign will have an effect on the length of the customer relationship—also negatively. In such cases, we discuss how you should handle this.

Another complexity that you must consider before assessing the value of a campaign is its purpose. You can, in general, divide campaigns into whether they are focused on formulating a specific offer, such as two cans of tomatoes for $2, or whether they are promoting the brand that produces the canned tomatoes. For campaigns that promote specific offers, it is relatively easy to measure their success for a limited period of time. Branding campaigns, however, potentially promote a wide series of products at the same time. Therefore, their effect can be harder to measure since they are less product specific, and the potential effects wear off over a longer period in a market that also can be very volatile.

This section shows how, through the use of customer analytics, you can make a business case comparison on a campaign level. Some might argue that volume-driven performance comparisons where we simply measure the number of units sold might be good enough. This could be true in a simple business landscape where there pretty much only is one go-to market approach. However, for most modern companies, there are multiple sales channels. Therefore, the price of the same pair of red shoes might be different depending on whether they are purchased in a physical store or on the Internet. Also the costs of selling the shoes are different since physical outlets typically are associated with higher costs per sales compared to Internet sites. If, however, this were the only pair of shoes that we would ever sell via the Internet site, this might be the most expensive pair of shoes your company ever sold.

Another advantage of the business case approach is that, based on an ROI evaluation, you can evaluate how best to spend your marketing budget. Perhaps you should close down some campaigns and focus more on customer acquisition or retention. Perhaps you should pass your budget on to the product development department, since this is where the money is best spent. Alternatively you might get an argument for why you should get an increased budget for the next season, which simply could be that the return is higher than your cost of lending capital.

The business case model presented in Exhibit 5.2 says that the costs of running a campaign are the up-front costs combined with the ongoing costs. On the benefit side, there will be increased revenues based on the customer's increased spending during the campaign

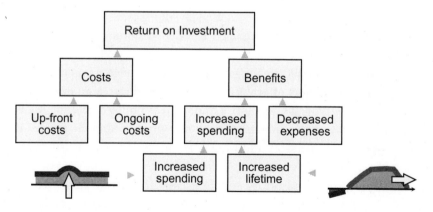

Exhibit 5.2 ROI Tree

period. Potentially this period can be for the rest of the customer's lifetime, and the customer's lifetime might be affected by the campaign. Campaigns can also result in decreased expenses if they educate customers in how to do self-service as a part of the offer. The rest of this section explains how you can estimate the different parameters in more detail.

Up-front costs are the costs associated with enabling the organization to launch the campaign in the first place. For a typical campaign, they might include the use of external partners in designing a creative universe or time spent by the organization doing this. It could be the fixed costs of producing promotional material, such as folders, radio spots, or letters. It could also be the costs of setting up information systems that monitor the effect of the campaign, software or information technology consultancy purchased specifically to enable these campaign activities. The training costs of your sales staff should also be included here along with the customer service or call center training costs.

As a rule of thumb, you should include only elements that are purchased just for this particular campaign. If your analytical department purchases a data-mining tool as a result of the company strategy, exclude this cost from your business case as the software would have been purchased under any circumstances and also will be used for other activities.

Ongoing costs are the costs that your company will have to carry for as long as the campaign or its effects last. These costs will include continuous training of staff, campaign management, maintaining material, responding to campaign-specific customer requests, and so on.

Ongoing costs typically include credit checks needed for customers who accepted the new offer if it exposes the vendor to a financial risk. Ongoing costs typically do not include a welcoming letter, if this is sent to all customers that purchased the given offer. Therefore, it is a variable cost per sales and is included in the revenue (turnover – variable costs).

Increased earnings can be more or less difficult to estimate based on how you track your lag information. This chapter gives only a brief presentation about how to do this. If you want to read more about this, see Chapter 7, which presents individual methodologies in greater detail.

If your campaigns are of an ongoing nature, the effects that you will track will have to do with the changing deployment of resources. You might have spent more or less on commercial or sales staff, or the offer and the price gap to the nearest competition might have varied over time. In this case you typically will use forecasting models to tell you which resource allocations that you have been using, alone and in combination with whatever other means, have given the highest return. Forecasting models also give you an indication about which effects have the fastest bottom-line impact.

In case your campaign is more of a one-off event, there will be no long line of historical data to learn from. You should consider estimating the effect of the campaign based on the difference between a "holdout sample" or a "parallel market" and your target group or target market. In this way you can validate whether the campaign had an effect if you assume that the control group or parallel market will behave as your target market would, had you not launched a campaign. From a statistical perspective, you would be searching for whether you sell significantly more in your target market compared to your control group or control market. In a very stable and predictable market, you can, of course, also consider not using control groups and benchmark your campaign results against the previous periods.

If you have a sales or customer relationship management (CRM) system, or procedures—and a culture—that can link additional sales to existing campaigns on an individual customer basis, it is a very simple mathematical exercise to sum up the increased earnings and allocate them to a given market activity.

Decreased expenses can be one of the side effects of a cross- or up-selling campaign. It is typically not the primary aim of such a campaign; rather, it is the purpose of campaigns aimed at reducing the costs of serving customer segments (described in great detail in Chapter 3).

In up-selling campaigns, relatively often some process improvement elements are embedded in the newer version of a service or a product. For example, the online service might now integrated as a

Exhibit 5.3 ROI for a Given Campaign

Costs		Benefits			
Up-front costs	Campaign costs per months	Growth in profit	Increased lifetime * base turnover	Decreased expenses	ROI
5,000 USD	2 * 3,000 USD	2 * 5,000 USD	3 * 1,000 USD	0 USD	18%

part of the software package, which might reduce the alternative use of a costly call center. Another example may be if you exchange your current mobile product for a newer one where you pay via direct debit; regardless of what more you get, the telecom company will also reduce its losses on bad debt and in this way decrease its expenses.

Exhibit 5.3 shows how the ROI could look for a single campaign. The campaign, executed through an external call center, could be promoting a new printer to small office customers. The up-front costs could be $5,000 for making scripts and preparing the call center sales agents, leaflets, and so on. The costs of running a two-month campaign could be $3,000 since you rent the sales agents on a day-to-day basis for as long as the new sales process lasts. The growth in profits could be $5,000 for the two months of the campaign, which includes the variable costs per sales, such as sending the product to the customer. From other campaigns and customer interviews, we know that a certain loyalty effect is a spinoff of such campaigns. This loyalty effect can be measured using survival analysis as presented in Chapter 4 in the section "Finding the Most Valuable Target Group." This loyalty effects has been estimated to add an additional three months to the average customer lifetime, and the average profit per customer in the customer base is $1,000 per month. The ROI is estimated to be 18% ((13,000 − 11,000)/11,000).

More advanced business case makers might want to estimate the net present value (NPV) of the campaign, which could be relevant for market activities lasting for long periods or effects kicking in over a longer term. Another argument for estimating the NPV is to compare the return of a cross-selling campaign with the effect of an acquisition campaign.

PROFILING TARGET GROUPS

In the previous section, you read about how to identify and select the campaigns that give you the highest returns from a business case perspective. See also Chapter 8. A second and very natural step after having identified the best campaigns is to improve them even more. This exercise was described in Chapter 4 in regard to acquisition processes. However, there is one big difference between the situation described in Chapter 4 and here, and it is all about the data.

In the acquisition campaigns discussed in Chapter 4, there would be relatively little customer data available to analyze, since we have little information about the prospects that were contacted and did not accept our offer. In the best case we would have the directory data that came with the lead lists, such as type of company, industry, numbers employed, turnover, and so on. When you are dealing with cross- and up-selling, you are building on an existing customer relation, which also means that you might have customer-specific data stored in your DW. Instead of having just directory information about where a customer lives or general information about what a company does, you might have information about what specific products and services each individual customer typically purchases, when they purchase, and through which channel they purchase. Also, you might have other types of information about what your customers like, what they find difficult from your call center logs, their ability and willingness to pay their bills on time from your dunning department, how often they change address, age of the person or the company, and so on.

In brief, therefore, as in Chapter 4, you can profile which customers typically responded positively to your historical campaigns and target their twins in your customer base that have not received the offer yet. As in Chapter 4, you should also consider how you can calibrate the campaign more specifically to this segment in order to increase the hit rate even more.

Less trained analysts view a DW full of opportunities more as a threat than as an advantage. The problem is that there simply is too much data and too many data definitions to learn. This is a tragic truth, since this also means that the more data that is made available, the less inclined some analyst will be to use it. It is also my experience that analysts with no statistical knowledge lack the tools and knowledge to handle large and complex data. One alternative is to consider whether these individuals can be trained to become analysts. Another is not to give them complex analytical tasks. A third and more appealing alternative is to create a customer mart that aggregates and presents data in a format these analysts can handle.

Making a Customer Base Table

Making a customer base table can be seen as a basic, unavoidable, and very first delivery for companies that want to do advanced CRM, customer intelligence, or customer analytics. This base table typically has one line per customer, contractual obligation, or company depending on industry. Exhibit 5.4 shows a simple example of what could be a fraction of an analytical base table. Imagine that this is how a base table looks for a telecom operator where one customer can have many subscriptions and where some data will be on a customer level (customer code) and other variables will provide information on a contract level (contract number).

The overall rule is, however, one line per commercial "target." Based on this input, an experienced customer analyst will spend a significant amount of time going through all available data sources and evaluating their relevance to all current and expected tasks. Practically this means that the analyst should look at each variable in all available data sources and consider how each can be implemented in the analytical base table. Exhibit 5.5 shows a usability versus availability plot. It is a simple graphical representation, on a data source level, of which data sources should be implemented in a customer base table. As you can see from the gray area in the plot, not all data sources will be included in the customer base table that we are about to create, since some data sources simply are not useful for the given tasks. In other cases the data simply is so hard to acquire that it is not worth the sourcing efforts.

Exhibit 5.5 also documents the whole idea of why a company should create a single enterprise-wide DW: It makes all the data available, including historical data, and typically also increases that usability of the data by adding business terms and rules to what would have

Exhibit 5.4 Analytical Base Table for Customer Analytics

Customer code	Customer age	Contract no.	Contract age	Speech/ min	Date/ MB	SMS/ count	MMS/ count	Download/ USD	Comsumption months-1	Comsumption months-2
a	33	1	23	32	0	467	53	0	96	84
a	33	2	33	23	2	0	0	0	23	12
a	33	3	1	44	0	0	0	0	34	33
b	12	1	12	237	0	64	2	0	55	67
c	45	1	32	72	3	3	0	12	34	29
d	23	1	21	55	3	2	0	34	45	70
d	23	2	4	115	1	43	0	45	74	55

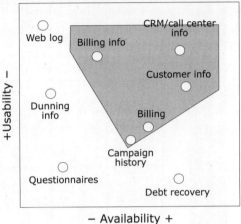

Exhibit 5.5 Usability versus Availability Plot

been a raw data dump from an operational system. Having all the data in one place also means that different data sources can be joined; this allows the organization to have one shared version of the truth. As they say: "It is not hard to make everybody work hard at the same time; the difficult thing is to make everybody pull in the same direction at the same time."

When you have identified which data sources that you want to include data from, the next step is to decide which particular variables to include in your customer base table. In general, the data has to live up to at least one of these requirements in order to be included:

- **The variable in the DW correlates with the target variable.** This means that if the variable can help explain or describe the difference between the group that accepted the offer and those that did not, then it should be included in data mart. During this stage, you should also consider whether you want to use the data mart for churn prediction, since doing so would give more target variables that could trigger the inclusion of individual variables.

- **The variable in combination with other variables correlates significantly with the target variable.** In this case we might find that an individual variable does not on its own correlate with the target variable(s); however, if it does correlate in combination with others, we might want to include it into our data mart.

- **The analyst believes that the variable will become useful in the future.**

- **It is general information used in the organization or expected to be used.** If the organization traditionally sees customers as divided into segments according to where they geographically have their home address, it would be a logical step also to include this information in the base table since sooner or later the analyst will be expected to use this definition in his or her work.

A customer mart should also be set up so that the analyst can use it for reporting on already existing campaigns. If we are using the base table to generate lead information, we might as well also set it up so we can create lag information from it. This way the analyst also ensures to the maximal extent that there is only one version of the truth, based on the same information used in the base table. This also provides considerable time savings; imagine a company that runs 33 campaigns at the same time and how many resources will be needed to track the performance of the individual campaigns if they are not based on a shared data foundation.

Another benefit from using a customer base table is that most ad hoc questions and one-time reports can be generated using it as a data foundation. Doing this saves a lot of resources for an analyst. An ad hoc inquiry can be solved in ten minutes using the base table as a data foundation; if the same data foundation had to be built from scratch via Structured Query Languages and data mergers, it typically would take from one hour to a full day. In many cases I have generated fact-based input during creative sessions, giving focus and direction to brainstorms as they were happening. This way of working actively supports the creative process with fact-based decision support. If you do not have a base table, the creative forums will have to wait for hours or days until they can get their fact-based decision support. Since they often cannot wait so long, they will simply go on without the data. In such cases, your investment in the customer analytics function has created no value and perhaps only potential frustration instead.

Also it is essential that all analysts share their data marts to ensure internal alignment in the way decision support is presented. It is not hard to imagine the frustration in the commercial organization if two different members of the same customer analytics department provide two different outputs when given the same task. Even though there will typically only be small differences in these reports, and the decisions based on the reports would be the same no matter which version were used, the credibility of the customer analytics function will be eroded. Also the commercial side of the organization will have to use one of the reports as a basis for its decisions, and it will of course use the one created by the analyst that it for some reason believes to be the most trustworthy and competent. Subconsciously, therefore, during this process they have evaluated the other analyst to be more or less incompetent. This alignment is even more crucial when the customer analytics function is divided between multiple geographical locations or when analysts work very independently with their tasks.

One of the dangers of this way of working is that the base tables take over as a primary source of organization-wide reporting and become seen as a competitor to ordinary DW reports. For the same reason there should be a feedback process from the customer analytics department to the business intelligence department regarding which dimension the organization would like to see reporting done through. Also you will have to train the organization in how to use the proper tools for standard reporting, which means that they should start pulling reports themselves and use the analytical resources only for innovation and complex analysis. Finally, a shared data mart is also an efficient way of ensuring that customer analytics competencies, on the data side, become dependent on individuals. It can reduce the break-in time of a new analyst from six to 12 months down to only between one to three months.

Next we turn back toward how to improve your CRM selling activities from a statistical perspective. Decision trees were presented in Chapter 4; they are used in the same way in this chapter. The only difference is the data foundation. In Chapter 4 it was about input from directories or the like, whereas here the data comes from the analytical base table. This enables more complex decision trees since there can be hundreds of variables in a base table. Having this many variables is essentially a luxury since it means that we can make additional, sophisticated profiles on customers we wish to target. However, it also raises the need for competent analysts.

Selecting the Right Algorithm

Before we go to the modeling phase, you must know the answer to one question: Do you want to know only which customers should be contacted, or do you also want to know why they should be contacted?

Before we answer this question, some words of reassurance. If you are reading all the exotic names of algorithms that can analyze data in different ways, you might believe that data mining is too difficult to handle.

There is no doubt that data mining takes time and requires certain analyst competencies. However, the most difficult part is setting up the right data in the right way; the next most difficult part is learning how to handle the algorithms. I say this based on the fact that when you do data-mining projects, typically you spend 40% of your time on getting data and presenting it right (which is why user-friendly software is essential for data mining projects), 30% on interviewing the organization about what the data means, 20% on convincing stakeholders that this is the right way to go (which is why a data miner should be more than an introverted number person), and only 10% or less on doing the actual modeling (the algorithm-specific competencies). You can gain the necessary, very basic modeling competencies in a two- to four-day course provided by leading analytical software vendors. If you have never seen how modeling is done, invite a sales representative to provide examples. As a starting point I suggest that you invite either SAS Institute or SPSS/IBM since they are market leaders in this field.

Going back to the initial question of this section, you might just want to know which customers have an increased propensity for purchasing a given product. In this case, you can use binary logistical regression, discriminant analysis, neural networks, decision trees, or other algorithms. The output of these algorithms will be an additional field in your base table that indicates how likely each of the customers would be, based on their current profile, to purchase a given offer.

From a work flow perspective, your project plan could be based on the steps presented in Exhibit 5.6. After making a customer base table (containing all your active customers as a minimum), the first step would be to select all the customers that have been targeted by a campaign promoting a specific offer and make a variable describing which of these customers accepted the offer. Now you can generate a data-mining model that identifies the characteristics of customers that accepted the offer (also known as profiling or modeling). The next step is to score the full customer mart. Use the model to identify other customers in your customer base similar to those that accepted the offer of the campaign and who, therefore, would be likely to accept the same offer during a future campaign. Using professional data mining tools, scoring all your customers will take approximately five minutes.

Perhaps you also want to know *why* these customers accepted the offer, which provides a work flow as shown in Exhibit 5.7. You can learn what makes a customer accept your offer if you use algorithms that are easier to interpret than binary regression analysis or neural networks. For example, decision trees can give you a profile of

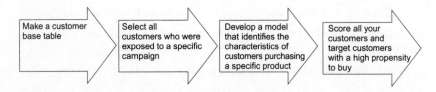

Exhibit 5.6 Improving Campaigns via Targeted Rollout

Exhibit 5.7 Improving Campaigns via Targeted Rollout and Communication

customers that typically accept the offer. With this knowledge at hand, you might want to target the product or service or simply the way that you convey the offer to fit the typical needs of customers with this profile.

As an example, try to imagine an SUV as the product to be sold. If you find that companies purchase the car, your message could focus on how the spacious car solves all needs of the traveling salesperson. If you find that young, single men in a wealthy area purchase it, perhaps you would stress that this car is cool looking with room for golf clubs. Alternatively, if the car typically is sold to young families, it could be marketed as a car that can move a family in a safe and organized manner with room for strollers, baby beds, extra clothing, toys, diapers, and the dog. The point here is that if you use decision trees or emphasize interpreting the model in any way, you will know both whom to target and potentially how. Such insight could be created from Exhibit 5.8, which indicates an increased purchase rate in the family segment with children.

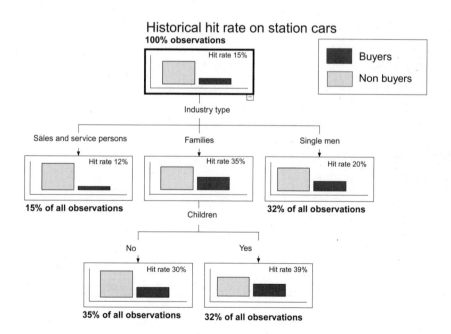

Exhibit 5.8 Segment Identification via Decision Trees

Other examples of what can come out of interpreting models could include:

- You get a clear profile of the target group and can, based on this knowledge, go from general marketing to targeting.

- You learn that a given product serves two or more segments and decide to target only some of these segments based on their expected future growth or expected customer lifetime.

- You learn about the target groups and decide to develop new customized products (more research will probably also be needed) and have, this way, started to use the input for product innovation.

- You do not find any patterns in the data and simply decide to offer the product to your entire customer base—unless they already have one.

If you want to work extensively with the model interpretation element, you should also consider using interactive decision trees since these give you the opportunity to move and define the different splits exactly as you would slice and dice in a pivot table. The difference is that decision trees give you statistical input on which dimension you should slice in order to concentrate on a specific quality defined by the target variable, in this case whether the customers did accept the offer or not. Also decision trees and the software that comes along with them will help you in evaluating the effects of targeting specific groups. This evaluation of the effects includes validating whether your segmentation model can be seen as representing your full customer base or whether the patterns you find simply are a result of some local phenomena only present in the data that you have analyzed. If you want to read more about decision trees and how to make campaigning based on them, you should read Chapter 6 about customer retention, the case study in Chapter 9, or Chapter 4 in my previous book, *Business Analytics for Managers*.[1]

GENERAL OFFERS BASED ON THE CUSTOMER PROFILES

You have been directed to this section if you indicated that you have customer level information across several transactions as you can imagine a bank has. A bank therefore knows who holds the shopping basket and can therefore analyze on a customer level. The opposite could be a traditional supermarket which does not know who holds that basket, only what is purchased together in a basket from the receipts saved through the cash registers. You have also indicated that either you want to launch a new campaign or that you have no campaigning history to build this campaign on.

The techniques used in this section are very similar to the ones used in the last section, "Profiling Target Groups." You should read that section first and then continue reading this one; which will only outline the minor differences between these two approaches. The concept of a customer-centric analytical base table was presented in the last section. This is a correct first step for any customer analytics function.

Here the difference is that you have no historical data on who was targeted via a campaign and who responded positively to it. You do, however, have information about which customers have purchased which offers. Based on this information, you can use an algorithm to help in identifying the characteristics of the customers who use a specific service or product. The only difference between what is presented here and what was presented in the last section is that here the models are developed across all the customers in your analytical base table, whereas in the last section the models were developed only on a subsample of the analytical base.

The model generated on the full customer base will be less exact, since it will include customers that have the purchaser profile but never did purchase the offer since they were never given the chance to do so. Such a customer, which could have been classified as a "Purchaser," since it might have accepted the offer if given the possibility, always will be classified as a "Nonpurchaser," which makes it harder for the algorithm to pick up the characteristics of a purchaser profile.

Apart from this, the rest of the process is the same; you can choose to focus only on which customers to target, which is the process described in Exhibit 5.9, excluding the gray arrow. Alternatively, you can choose an algorithm that also allows you to interpret and interactively optimize the model according to what is optimal for your

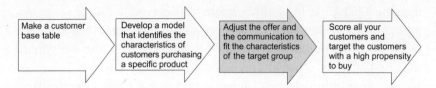

Exhibit 5.9 Simple Campaigns Based on Profiling

organization rather than according to what is statistically optimal. Since many organizations have what is known as product managers (individuals responsible for a named range of products and services), it would be natural to select your algorithm after having had discussions with the product managers.

PROMOTION OF REPLACEMENT OFFERS

If you used the decision tree in the beginning of this chapter (Exhibit 5.1), you have been directed to this section because you have knowledge about what your customer purchases over time and you want to promote a replacement offer to an existing customer base. The aim of a replacement campaign is to offer customers an upgrade of an existing product. This means that if customers respond positively to your campaign, they are expected to swap their existing service or product for another one. An example could be mobile or fixed phone replacement programs in the telecom industry, upgrades on seats in an airplane, a newer car for a family, an updated software version, and new types of loans in a bank.

Identifying Replacement Offers Using Your Base Table

If you are in an industry where replacement offers are essential, this fact will be reflected in the analytical base table that you have produced, as shown in Exhibit 5.10. Here the current and historical products purchased are presented per customer. If the data is presented in this way, all you have to do is to combine the fields "Current product" and "Previous product" into a third field. A simple frequency table would in this case reveal that customers that currently use

Exhibit 5.10 Base Table for Replacement Products

Customer code	Customer age	Contract no.	Current product	Previous product	Combined field
a	33	1	A	M	AM
a	33	2	B		B
a	33	3	G	K	GK
b	12	1	D	D	DD
c	45	1	S	D	SD
d	23	1	A	M	AM
d	23	2	A	M	AM

product A typically were users of product M before. The next thing you would like to do as an analyst is to identify those customers that still use product M and promote product A to them. You could also use the same techniques as presented in the "Profiling Target Groups" section, in order to identify whether your future campaign should be directed to more than one segment and to get some insight regarding the characteristics of the target group or groups.

Identifying Replacement Offers Using Transactional Tables

Most data mining tools also have pattern detection algorithms, which can perform the same task as shown in Exhibit 5.11 as well as many other complexities. Consider these complexities:

- If based on a timestamp variable, you want to analyze transactional purchases that happened within a certain time period or determine if the time interval between the transaction should be limited in some way. This could occur if you consider a customer to have been lost if more than two years pass between purchases. For example, if you are selling fertilizer to farmers, such products typically are purchased every season.

Exhibit 5.11 Replacement Data Presented for Pattern Detection Algorithms

Contract no.	Product	Date
a1	X	01-03-2008
a1	M	18-05-2009
a1	A	01-03-2010
a2	B	05-06-2007
a3	K	06-03-2007
a3	G	01-06-2008
b1	D	23-09-2009
b1	D	19-05-2010
c1	D	22-05-2010
c1	S	30-05-2010

- If you sell two different telephones to the same customer within two weeks, you probably would not see this as a traditional replacement action but more like a case of a broken mobile phone, a customer buying the wrong phone and replacing it, or because one of the phones will be given to someone else.

- You can direct pattern detection algorithms regarding how long the repurchase pattern should be. In some instances it might be of interest to see strings of three (AMX) rather than just the last purchase (AM).

- You also could focus on which product was purchased first, since this would indicate which acquisition offers grew into which off-the-shelf offers. This knowledge can have great impact on your customer acquisition processes, since if you acquire customers with low-yielding product and afterward they still do not want to purchase offers that would make them profitable, you have to revisit the way you do acquisitions since the current way is a dead end.

- Algorithms can be forced to suppress minor purchase patterns in order for the analysis to focus on the important ones.

If you would like to work more extensively with pattern or sequence detection algorithms, the data typically has to be presented as in a transaction log, meaning one line per transaction, and then sorted by customer and when the transaction occurred.

The benefit of this method is that you will be able to predict which customers should be offered which upgrade without having to spend a lot of time on analyzing tables and customer profiles. This could be relevant in the furniture industry or travel industry, where there are many and constantly changing trends and where the last purchase or destination will have a significant effect on the next purchase. You should, however, always be aware of the timing of the new offer, since if a customer has just bought a sofa, he or she is not likely to buy another one within a week and may feel intimidated if a new one was promoted to him or her this soon.

The same is true in the travel industry, where the time factor also is relevant since customers tend to purchase longer and more exotic trips during summer holidays than they do between holidays, where a typical trip is a three-day trip to a capital or specific site over a weekend. All in all, analysts should therefore sometimes not only generate information about what a customer should be offered but also when the offer should be promoted, something that product managers also are likely to stress.

COMPETING ON WALLET SHARE

If you used the decision tree in the beginning of this chapter (see Exhibit 5.1), you were directed to this section because you have knowledge about what your customer purchases over time and you are operating in an industry where many of your customers often use more than one supplier. The characteristics of your industry could therefore be that it is commoditized, there are many suppliers, or there are low switching costs or low costs associated with a multisourcing strategy for customers. This could be in the retail industry, where consumers often use more than one supermarket or outlet, or the air travel industry, where transactional customers often compare offers from several companies before deciding which one to accept.

Wallet Share Estimation Based on External Data Sources

The purpose of this analysis is to estimate the actual wallet share per customer (the percentage of a customer's total spending within your business area that is awarded to your business) and then, based on the results, try to capture the remaining wallet share from your competitors. This is often an easy way of increasing your market volume since you already have a relationship with the customers that you will be focusing your campaign on. The ultimate goal is, of course, to become the sole vendor to each of your customers, even if doing so requires some discount, simply because the competition might be working on the same type of campaign—so you had better be first.

This section assumes that your company has a DW that can reveal the consumption or turnover per customer, so getting this sort of data should be relatively simple. The difficult part is to estimate the total spent within your business area per customer, since this is the second part of what we need to know in order to estimate the wallet share per customer:

$$\text{Your customer wallet share} = \frac{\text{Customer spending in your business area awarded to your business}}{\text{What the customer spends in total in the same business area}}$$

To estimate the total spent per customer within your business area, often you have to use external data sources to calculate the total consumption per customer. External data sources in the shipping industry could be the *Journal of Commerce*, a database where you can see exactly how many containers specific organizations ship in and out of the United States, including whether they use other shippers.

If you are targeting business customers in the telecom industry, there will be no data on the total telecom consumption on a company level. You could potentially estimate a customer's total spending using directory information. You can take two steps to do so.

1. Identify a series of customers within a range of industries for which you know you are the only vendor. From the directory data, you can identify how many people are employed in the given firms and then estimate the average consumption per employed person based on your own DW data.

2. With this knowledge, combined with directory information about how many employed persons there are in all the firms of your customer base, you will be able to estimate your wallet share. If the average consumption in the production industry is one subscription per three employees, for example, and you have sold the company only one per every six employees, this indicates that the company uses another vendor. You should inform your sales agent of this.

Obviously, the precision of such estimates can be very uncertain. This uncertainty can be reflected in the way that such a solution eventually is implemented, which could be by entering the estimates into the sales management system and then freely allowing the salesperson responsible to overwrite it if he or she is certain that there are no other suppliers. Estimation of wallet share will, however, also on other occasions redirect the focus toward customers that otherwise could have been lost or have great selling potential. At the same time you can establish wallet share reporting per industry, which can drive the focus of your organization in this direction.

Wallet Share Estimation Based on Questionnaires

Another way to estimate the wallet share is simply to ask customers and enter their responses into the analytical base table. Since it is unlikely that you will get a 100% response rate, you can develop a prediction model that can score all your customers based on the responses that you have been given. In case you just want an estimate per customer, you can use neural networks and the scoring of the base mart data should be done in a day or two.

If you know that there are large differences between distinct customer groups, you should make a neural network per customer group, which will not add much complexity to the score back exercise.

Alternatively, still assuming that you are working with distinct customer groups, you can consider using interactive decision trees, where you force the algorithm to make the first splits according to your business logic. The reason for splitting data according to business logic is that if you make a neural network, the effect in one group will spill over on other groups—which is also why you should make one neural network per group. If you use decision trees, the effects of what happens within one branch will not spill over into the other branches, so you can isolate the differences within the groups. The ability to isolate effects within branches can be considered a strength of decision trees, yet it is also a weakness since decision trees rapidly get to a point where the samples become too small to work with statistically; every time you make a simple split in a decision tree, you decimate the data available for the next split. You can compensate for this weakness by boosting the decision tree (via a simple click in leading software packages), meaning that you can make an additional decision tree, or a series of them, that focus on explaining all the misclassified cases. In this way you allow variables other than the few most dominant ones (used in the previous trees) to have an effect on how a case should be classified. This concept of continuously adding a model that can explain what the previous model could not also works with neural networks. Within these neural networks the additional models are called layers, but the purpose is to explain the remaining patterns (residual information) in data, and layers will be added to layers until there is nothing left but random variation between what the model seeks to explain and all the input variables.

Which method is best is determined by the precision of the models. Therefore, you should compare the performance of the two model types on a data set different from the one that the statistical model was developed from. This is the most common way to evaluate models in data mining. You take all your responses and divide them into two data sets. On the first data set, you develop your models. On the second data set, you compare the model's ability to predict. The use of a second data set (also known as an evaluation data set) is needed to be sure that whatever patterns the algorithm has detected are universal for the population, not just characteristics of the specific sample that your model is based on.

Wallet Share Estimation Based on Loyalty Programs

One fascinating example of how wallet share estimation can be used is a European supermarket where you can sign in to a loyalty club. During registration, you also indicate how many children you have, their age and gender, and whoever else might live with you. Since you use your club card every time you shop to get your discounts, the supermarket can estimate your "stomach share" (how many calories have been purchased in the supermarket compared to how many are needed to maintain a standard family of the size indicated). If this stomach share is less that 100%, it is assumed that the customer also shops somewhere else. The chain also, based on information about what has been purchased, can identify the types of consumption items bought elsewhere and start promoting them via individual emails to the customer. In this way the supermarket identifies both whom to target and what to offer.

Wallet Share Estimation Based on Consumption over Time

You do not necessarily have to use complex algorithms and external data sources to estimate your customers' wallet shares, since sudden drops in demand from individual customers, depending on the industry, strongly indicate that they have started to source from elsewhere. In this case, it is the drop rather than an estimate of the total spending that triggers a customer audit. For the same reason, this way of monitoring your customer base should be seen as being complementary, or if you will, just another element that can trigger some actions from your sales staff.

PROMOTING BUNDLED OFFERS

If you used the decision tree in the beginning of this chapter (see Exhibit 5.1), you were directed to this section because you have knowledge about what your customers purchase and are in a market where you can sell more products and services to them at the same time. In order to do this analysis, you must know what is being purchased together (generally speaking, what can be found in the same shopping basket per customer visit). Sometimes you also know who holds the basket, but even if you do not, you still can learn about what products should be co-promoted, placed together in stores, or bundled and presented as a new product.

Bundling Using Cluster Analysis

If you use a cluster analysis for bundling your products, you will get not only a series of product combinations that goes well together but also a segmentation model that divides your customers into distinct groups according to their user needs. To do this sort of analysis, you should have knowledge on a customer level: which customers purchase what, and some sociodemographic data for all customers in order to be able to describe the clusters afterward. You can read more about how to make a cluster analysis on DW data in Chapter 4 in the section "Needs-Based Segmentation Created from Data Warehouse Data." Here is a brief summary of the four-step process.

1. Recode the data so that there is one variable per product or service and one line per customer.

2. Set the new variables so that if a customer has purchased a product, this variable will score 1; if not, 0.

3. Run a hierarchical cluster analysis on the data, identify natural groupings, and add background data onto the groups to validate the model and provide additional insight about the latent customer needs that form these purchasing patterns.

4. If the cluster analysis does not come up with a useful segmentation model, then you can run a principal component analysis (PCA) on all the variables describing which products the individual customers have purchased. This will give a series of new variables that represent purchase patterns. Afterward you can run a cluster analysis on the factor scores (the output variables of the PCA analysis described earlier as purchase patterns). This will simplify the picture and possibly help the cluster algorithms to identify some patterns. How to run a PCA (also known as an exploratory factor analysis) is described in detail in Chapter 4

in the section "Needs-Based Segmentation Created from Questionnaire Data."

Bundling Using Principal Component Analysis

If you still do not get any clear results from your cluster analysis, you can consider whether the result of the PCA in itself is a useful input. For example, an analysis of the purchasing habits in a British supermarket showed that frozen pizza, canned beer, and baked beans very often could be found together in customers' baskets. A PCA on this data would come up with one unique dimension that would correlate highly with all the three product types.

The next step in the analysis would be to examine which background variables score highly on the beer/pizza/beans dimension. Not surprisingly, we would find this to be high age, single status, and gender equal to male. Alternatively, you can use decision trees to identify the characteristics of this customer group by making a target variable that is equal to one for all customers that have purchased all three products in combination and using the sociodemographic variables as input variables.

What the supermarket now can do is to place these three items next to each other in a place where the target groups would be expected to pass by. Since there are frozen products involved, this speaks to moving the other products to the frozen foods section of the store. In this way the supermarket can remind the relevant male customers to buy all the products and teach others about this exotic food mix. The supermarket also has the opportunity to bundle the products into one offer or alternatively place beers that provide a higher yield than those typically sold next to the pizza.

Bundling Using Visual Analysis and Decision Rules

In some instances or industries, data exists only on a basket level, meaning that all the organization knows is what was purchased together—typically from the cash register. In this case, where there is no data that identifies who carries the shopping baskets, you will not have any sociodemographic data to add to your analysis; neither do

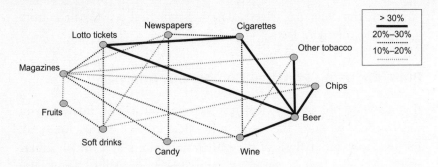

Exhibit 5.12 Visual Basket Analysis

you have any knowledge about frequency of purchases or the development of the consumption patterns on a customer level.

In this case you should consider using what is known as basket or receipt analysis. In its simplest form, this analysis visualizes the relationships among products that can be found in the same basket.

Exhibit 5.12 is an example of such a basket analysis among 11 products that can be found in a typical kiosk. Depending on the software, when making these plots, users can define the type of line that should be drawn between the individual products, given how often they can be found in the same record. A record can be on a customer level if we have this information or on a receipt level if we only have data on transaction (basket) level.

In the examined data set, we find that lotto tickets, beer, and cigarettes typically are purchased together. We can also see that beer purchasers very often also buy chips, other kinds of tobacco, and wine. The plot can also tell us what things the customers do not purchase together—fruits and cigarettes; these items should not be bundled together.

Exhibit 5.12 is very basic. If you have several hundred product lines, some software packages can use maps that place associated products close to each other while making lines between the products and giving more specific information about the one-to-one relationships.

Instead of having complementary products identified via data visualization, analytical software also can produce a list of associated products, where each line in the table represents a decision rule (e.g., if a customer buys chips, he or she is 23% more likely also to purchase beer). Analytical software typically can score the data according to decision rules. In this way you get a prediction about what the next purchase will be; this is very useful if you know who the customer is.

Bundling Used on the Web

Bundling on the web is made up of the sort of algorithms that typically are used on Internet pages selling electronics, where you as a customer always are asked whether you would also like to purchase some extra batteries or a memory card of a certain kind along with your original purchase—whatever activates this decision rule. It is not hard to imagine how this bundling could add benefit to service industries, such as restaurants, hotels, and holiday resorts, where offers can be created continuously according to what service or meal the customer just ordered. In the near future, we also should expect communicating shopping carts that will remind customers that "According to the products you currently have in your cart, you are about to make a banana split soon. Please also consider using our white chocolate sauce, which is on special this week" or "Other people who purchase the ingredients for a banana split typically also buy diet food for the day after."

If you can link this data to individual customer profiles, you can use basket analysis to predict what a customer might be expected to buy the next time he or she visits the store or the Internet page. The methodology would be the same: Find products that typically are purchased together and promote them to customers who have not bought them yet. Alternatively, based on a basket analysis, you can bundle products and promote them to customers with relevant profiles.

GROWTH CAMPAIGNS BASED ON QUESTIONNAIRE DATA AND WORKSHOPS

If you used the decision tree in the beginning of this chapter (see Exhibit 5.1), you were directed to this section because you do not have a useful data foundation. You should now consider which of the different analytical approaches presented in this chapter you would prefer if you could get data from a DW. When you have identified this, the next thing you should consider is whether you can recreate the same or a similar data foundation via a survey and make the presented analysis? If yes, you should consider doing so. If not, you are likely to be better off interviewing subject matter experts, skipping the statistical analysis and going straight for the conclusions. At the end of the day, the source of your decision support is not as important as the fact that it is right.

Chapter 4 discusses what you should consider when designing a questionnaire and presents an example of a questionnaire that is useful primarily in industries selling complex products in a competitive market. That chapter also presents some good advice on how to manage a workshop with subject matter experts, which can help you identify a needs-based segmentation model, possibly avoiding the need for a survey or possibly as preparation for one.

If you choose to launch a questionnaire and use some of the analytical techniques presented in this chapter to sort the data, you should read the section about what to consider when creating a questionnaire in Chapter 3, since sometimes there is more to it that just generating a data set. Also you should read "Segmentation and Data Warehousing" in Chapter 1, which discusses the pros and cons of using questionnaire data versus DW data.

SEEING THE CRM SELLING PROCESS FROM A DYNAMIC PERSPECTIVE

This chapter is about how to make and use lead information for CRM selling processes and is structured according to how your organization is set up to do these processes, as illustrated in Exhibit 5.13. Based on the data you have available, customer analytics will, to a varying extent, be able to create value for your organization. Therefore, you must invest in data before you can harvest the full benefits from customer analytics.

Whether you should invest in customer analytics as a starting point or not is essentially a strategic question for your organization. Look into your organizational or marketing strategy and identify

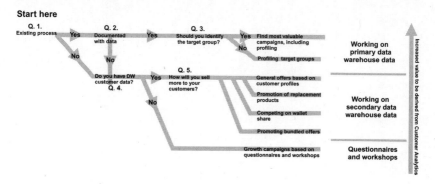

Exhibit 5.13 Improving Your Lead Information for Acquisition Processes

whether customer analytics can make your organization meet its strategic objectives. If you find that customer analytics could enable your organization to meet its strategic objectives, investigate where in Exhibit 5.13 you should be and where you are. Based on the discrepancies that you find, you will also get a clear indication about what challenges lay ahead of you.

You should also consider reading Chapter 8, which provides some strategic tools that will enable you to analyze your organization's current maturity level regarding customer analytics from an overall CRM/marketing process perspective.

NOTE

1. Gert Laursen and Jesper Thorlund, *Business Analytics for Managers: Taking Business Intelligence beyond Reporting* (Hoboken, NJ: John Wiley & Sons, 2010).

CHAPTER **6**

Lead Information for Customer Retention

If I told you which of your customers will leave you and when and why—would that be of any interest to you?

Before you start reading this chapter, remember the concept of this book. Chapter 2 is aimed for readers with strategic responsibilities whereas Chapters 3 through 7 are written primarily for project managers and customer analysts. Chapters 1, 8, and 9 are relevant to both user groups. This chapter focuses on where customer analytics becomes reality in the form of concrete analytical methods and data sources. Therefore, it may appear a bit technical for some.

This chapter is about how you can use customer analytics to increase the average customer life. Since this can be done in many ways, depending on the maturity of your information systems, in the beginning of this chapter we present a guide that leads you to a section that might serve as relevant inspiration for you, taking your current situation into account. Each of the next sections focus on the relationship among data, analytical methodology, and how you can integrate the results into the way that you do business. If you would like to read more about change management, stakeholder management, conflict resolution, and the like, read the first half of Chapter 3 as inspiration.

Either you are reading this book from one end to the other or you are reading this chapter because Chapter 2 recommended that you do so. Strategic or functional reasons for focusing on selling to the existing customer base could include:

- Your objectives clearly indicate that your success is directly linked to your ability to retain existing customers.

- Your customer base is declining either because your markets are maturing or your competitiveness is not up to date.

- You are placed in sales with responsibility for what happens after the contract is closed.

- You never before have worked actively with customer retention and there are potentially some quick wins in entering this high-value virgin territory.

- You are strategically positioned in a market with a relatively high penetration rate compared to expected market potential and the market has relatively disloyal customers.

- You as a product manager are responsible for introducing new products. This methodology will give clear input on how to design and introduce retention offers.

- Your company is the market leader and does not pursue growth either via market or product differentiation but is pursuing growth via a digging-in strategy.

There might be other reasons for focusing on retention activities, including that fact you simply just have to do on a continuous basis as a company. You might also have been given this focus as a result of your company strategy, where increasing volume per customer is a specified tactical maneuver. Alternatively this may be a decision of your own or coming from within your department as a functional strategy that you must execute successfully in order to meet some strategic objectives. Under all circumstances, you are now in a situation where you need to know how well customer analytics can give you guidance about how you can increase the customer loyalty through retention or win-back activities.

This chapter is about how you work with and generate *lead* information *before* creating a new retention campaign for your customers. The concept of lead information was described in Chapter 1. In brief, however, lead information describes the type of information that you, as commercial department, require in order to take to the next level a new or existing retention processes.

You should also read Chapter 7, which focuses on how to create and work with *lag* information. (Lag information is distinct in the sense that it is used to monitor and optimize within the framework of an existing process.) Lag information is therefore something you work with *while running* campaigns. Finally, you should also read Chapter 8 about *learning* information, which explains how you can use customer analytics systematically for organizational learning *after running* a campaign.

BEFORE YOUR CAMPAIGN

This section describes a series of analytical options, based on the series of assumptions closely linked to your objectives and the maturity of your organization. In general, customer analytics is heavily associated with business intelligence and use of data warehouse (DW) data, particularly when it comes to customer retention. In this chapter we also discuss the use of subject matter experts and questionnaires as data sources, simply *because customer intelligence should not be defined by where the data comes from but by the type of decision support that it enables.* See Chapter 1 for a more detailed discussion. This chapter promotes different analytical methodologies that can be used at different times with no limitation on where the data is sourced. The chapter also promotes a path of how to become better at using more information in the way you do marketing.

You can either choose to read the full chapter for inspiration, or you can go to the parts of the chapters that you find the most relevant. In all cases, you should, however, read the section "Introduction to Customer Retention" as an introduction to the subject. Exhibit 6.1 can give you some indication about which section to read afterward, if you choose only to read selected sections. Start using the decision tree in the upper left corner. Based on your response to the next three

Start here

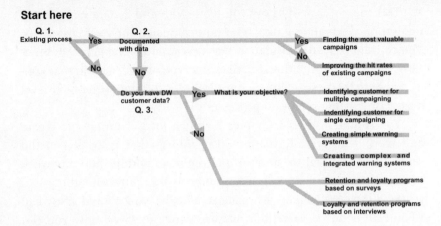

Exhibit 6.1 Chapter Structure

questions, you will get direction about what is likely to be relevant for you. The three questions are:

1. **Do you wish to optimize your already existing landscape of retention processes?** The purpose of this question is to uncover whether the retention campaign is something you have done before or currently are doing. If this is a new process, there cannot be any historical data to support your analytical efforts. If it is a known process, then you might have a lot of performance data to learn from.

2. **If this is not a new process, does data exist about the process?** If the answer is no, then from a customer analytics perspective you are as well off as if you had to establish this process for the first time. If the answer is yes, there might exist some usable lag information describing the historical performance of the campaigns that you can work with analytically and turn into lead information. Through this lead information, you can identify which processes are more successful and should be maintained or expanded. Also you can learn how to improve already existing retention campaigns.

3. **Do you have DW customer data?** Even though you do not have any historical data on current retention processes because they are new, data is not stored, or this simply is not the scope

of your task, DW information still can be used for retention purposes. If you have useful DW data, you can select whether you want to:

a. Create multiple campaigns (which is how a marketing department typically uses churn prediction).

b. Create a single campaign (which is how a call center typically uses churn prediction).

c. Create simple warning systems (which is how a sales function typically uses churn prediction).

d. Create a complex and integrated warning system (which is how a cross-functional or process excellence department typically uses churn prediction).

Alternatively you might still want to work with retention and loyalty programs based on questionnaire and subject matter expert input. This section also provides you with input if you are launching retention programs for the first time or if you simply want to take your retention program to the next level.

You can go straight to the recommended section based on where you find your organization's situation in the decision tree. You should also read Chapter 7, which discusses what to do *during* the campaign, and Chapter 8, which suggests what you could consider doing *after* the campaign. Chapter 9 is a case study of how a retention strategy was rolled out successfully. The next section gives a general introduction to the concept of customer retention from a customer analytics perspective.

INTRODUCTION TO CUSTOMER RETENTION

The objective of customer retention is to grow your customer base by not losing customers. The alternative is to launch acquisition campaigns and then grow your customer base that way. There are, however, arguments that speak for retention as opposed to acquisition activities:

- **You know what you have got, and you do not know what you get.** If you can estimate the value of your existing customers, you also know the ones that are of great value to your organization. An acquisition campaign can be compared to fishing with a big net; some of the customers that you catch will be profitable and some will be less so. This is also why in Chapter 2 we recommend that you target retention activities toward high-value customers as a starting point.

■ **Typically, it is cheaper to hold on to a customer than it is to go out and acquire a new one.** Again, the use of value-based segmentation will give you an overview on how much you can spend on retention offers to a specific customer.

■ **Customers over time are cheaper to serve since they need less support.** Loyal customers will also, to an increasing extent, act as ambassadors for your business and be willing to pay higher premiums. Also, it is a generally accepted fact that happy and loyal customers increase the attractiveness of working in your organization, which in turn reduces employee turnover and is reflected back on your brand.

Churn

Churn is a well-established term within retention. It describes the percentage of customers or contracts that are lost in a given period. This term is widely used in subscription-based markets, such as banking, insurance, telecom, fitness clubs, labor unions, and other member-based organizations.

Before you proceed with this chapter you should be aware that customers churn or get churned for many reasons. In order to make an effective retention strategy, you have to be aware that all these kinds of churn cannot be handled in the same way. Typical churn reasons are:

■ **Happy churn.** This churn describes the mood of customers that have left your organization yet were profoundly satisfied with what you provided to them. In this case you should either seek to win them back after they have left or predict when they typically will leave your company and send them a retention offer just before.

- **Unhappy churn.** This churn describes customers that were dissatisfied with your service and left your organization because of this. In this case, you should identify which processes failed and repair them before you lose more customers. Afterward you can run a win-back campaign toward the lost customers and promote the new and improved business processes to them supported by some sort of compensation.

- **Fraudulent churn.** This type of churn is created by customers that have engaged in a relationship with your organization only to get the acquisition offer or some other benefits without the intention of paying all their debts. The way to reduce this kind of churn is to prevent these persons or organizations from becoming customers in the first place and to minimize potential risks in the early phases of the customer relationship. These customers must never become active customers of yours a second time.

- **Churn caused by external factors.** At times churn can be caused by factors beyond your control. For example, if you find that you are losing customers in Spain due to a drastic decline in local market activities, then it is not a question of launching retention campaigns, winning back customers, or repairing any local processes. In this case, you should consider whether you should pull out of the local market or how to make sure that these customers will contact you again the next time the market allows them to use your services.

- **Base churn.** Other factors cause churn, such as bankruptcies among your customers or customers moving to other countries or ceasing to exist due to other reasons. This kind of churn is often referred to as base churn, which indicates the minimal customer churn rate that your organization can hope to achieve.

Elements Needed for Churn Prediction

This section describes the generic elements that have to be defined regardless of which DW-driven churn prediction approach you choose in relation to Exhibit 6.2. The first is a churn definition, which from

Exhibit 6.2 Generic Steps within Churn Prediction

a data perspective will define the target variable that your churn prediction model will pivot around. The section also provides good advice and a work plan for how you can efficiently build an analytical base table that can identify which customers you are at high risk of losing.

Define Churn

When does a customer churn? The rule is that churn occurs when you first received a notice from the customer and not, for example, when the subscription technically was closed down the following month when the notice period was over. This also means that some customers that you define as churners never actually did churn, which you should consider to be good news and ignore, since what you want to know is which customers have the intention of churning. If you miss out on this first rule, two things might happen:

1. You are about to develop a churn prediction model that is optimized to identify the customer you cannot save anyway.

2. You might put yourself in a situation where you will have to wait an additional month before you know who actually left, which is the same as losing business agility and the customers that left in the meantime.

In some markets, such as the shipping industry, customers do not hand in a message defining when they leave, they simply stop trading with your company, partially or completely. In such instances, you might define a churning customer as a company that gave you significantly less than half the expected trade. The big trick here is to define what is the expected trade, since some customers might be seasonal (e.g., fruits and nuts, etc.), and then you have to compare with the last year's activities during the same period. Alternatively you might simply compare last month's activity with the month before and see whether it has been reduced. Also you can consider estimating the average activity per customer and the corresponding standard deviation, and look for significant changes only. The ways of defining churn are endless. This churn definition is an essential first step for the success of all your succeeding activities, so do not rush this part of the exercise and make sure that all your commercial stakeholders agree with you. A very pragmatic approach to this problem could be to develop several churn definitions and then later hone in on the one definition or the combination that yields the best results during the modeling phase.

It is also important that you consider the "churn window": Should it be one month or two? The right window size has to do with having enough churner profiles to give a statistically reliable picture of what is going on in your customer database. Yet you might be at risk of missing out on the most recent trends in the market if you wait for three months of data until you launch your next model. A mix model could be to make a churn window for three months and still run the model once a month while possibly adding more weight to last month's profiles.

In cases where you have too few incidences to make a churn prediction model based on a traditional time window, you can treat all the churners you have registered in your data set as if they churned last month, including updating all the input variables so that if an event happened one month before, the customer churned. In this way you are taking the absolute time out of the equation while still maintaining the relative time between events.

Explore Churn Types and Churn Reasons

After having set the churn definition (also known within data mining as your output or target variable), and assuming that you also have created the data foundation, the next step is to generate the input variables that can explain why customers left. These variables then can be used for predicting which individual customers are likely to leave in the near future and which are not. A very obvious first step, which often is forgotten by technically oriented analysts, is to make full use of the knowledge already existing in your organization on what causes customers to churn. This could include making surveys and contacting customers that have left or in any other way expressed dissatisfaction with your services or products. As mentioned earlier, since there are many kinds of churn, your focus should be on which products or services did they use (looking for happy churn). Which processes did the customers use just before they left, and what was the process performance, such as errors in your bills to them, or what complaints do customers typically raise, such as dissatisfaction with the attitude of your call center agents (looking for unhappy churn)? Essentially you are looking for all the customer interaction points that there are.

Identifying Potential Data Sources

The next step is mapping which of your information systems can provide data about the relevant customer touch points identified. This is high-level analysis, identifying which systems you want to source data from one way or the other. As shown in the section "Profiling Target Groups" in Chapter 4, the general rule is that the selected data repositories should be relatively accessible and provide relevant information in order to be first priority for your project. Sometimes you might not have any information systems that can provide input to your model, such as in how friendly a manner customers feel that call center agents treat them. In this case you must consider whether you can make such a variable through automated exit surveys or the like, whether you can create a surrogate measure based on customer relationship management (CRM) data (Did the customer call the support line again with the same issue?), or whether you simply live without this information.

Add Variables to the Analytical Base Table

The next step is to identify the individual variables in the data repositories that you wish to include in your data mart. Sometimes the variables can simply be aggregated on a customer level and appended to your analytical base table. At other times some manipulation is needed, as shown in Exhibit 6.3, which presents a case from a telecom

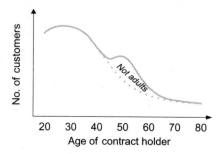

Exhibit 6.3 Business Logic Based on Assumptions

operator where customers must be adults in order to open a contract. This also means that even though a parent holds the contract, the phone is being used by a child, who might at some point churn for some reason. Particularly since younger persons are more easily influenced by commercials and media—which is why most commercials are aimed at them in the first place—this customer group requires extra surveillance.

One way of identifying such a group could be by looking for a hump at the age distribution of the customer base. This hump indicates the age band of the parents that hold contracts on behalf of their children. The next step is then to identify who within this age band are parents and who are children. In this case text messaging usage was a strong indicator. Based on this, we developed a business rule saying that if the contract is owned by someone in the age band between 40 and 60 and uses SMS relatively often, then the estimated age of the contract owner would be set to less than 18.

Other variables that can be good predictors in markets where you compete on wallet share are those that express customers' consumption trends over time, since this typically can indicate whether customers are to an increasing extent sourcing services or products from another vendor. The general rule for including variables in your data mart should be:

- The variable correlates significantly with the churn variable.
- The variable in combination with other variables correlates significantly with the churn variable, as in Exhibit 6.3.

- The variable measures a customer interaction point that is expected to become significant in the future.

- The variable represents a reporting dimension typically used by the company and therefore is likely to be required in future reporting.

If analysts are relatively new in the company, they must be in continuous contact with subject matter experts from the technical side of the organization to understand the data universes that they are sourcing from. Analysts also must consult with subject matter experts on the commercial side of the organization to learn and confirm the relevance of recent findings in the data. For this reason, analysts with technical, business, and interpersonal skills are required, which is a combination rarely found.

Select Algorithm

The final exercise for analysts is to decide what sort of algorithm to use for the data-mining process. Regardless of which algorithm is used when the churn prediction model become stabilized, it is strongly recommended that decision trees are used in the early parts of the development process and for evaluating the models. Decision trees will reveal logical errors, such as the one in a churn prediction model presented to me by some consultants who proudly claimed that, using neural networks, they could identify, nearly to the point, on a one-to-one basis which customers that were about to leave. Had they used decision trees, they would have noticed that the model entirely relied on a field saying that the customer had canceled the contract, which then, correctly enough, churned the next months. However, that is not really something you need a churn prediction model to tell you.

Another example was a churn prediction model I built which indicated at an early stage that none of the customers that had received a recent campaign had churned. Unfortunately, it was not a case of the perfect loyalty campaign. The case was that there were too few churners in the data set for the last many months; therefore, I recoded the data set as if they all had churned last month—working with relative rather than absolute time. This also meant that customers who in reality had churned five months ago could not have been exposed to that particular campaign; whereas the active customers that I was comparing the churners with all had received that recent campaign. The campaign had nothing to do with it, but the fact that churn could have happened a long time ago had *everything* to do with it. The point is that mistakes like these will be uncovered if you use decision trees, which point out what the models react to. Based on personal experience, I would say that if you find that you got your full data repository right the first time, it is just because you have not found the bugs yet.

How to Set Up the Data

The first time that you as an analyst set up the data flow for churn prediction, you will find it to be somewhat head-spinning. The principle is that we will profile the characteristics of last month's churners—called making a model—and assume that the customers who today have these characteristics also are likely to churn within the next month. As you can see from Exhibit 6.4, you will have to generate a historical data set (called historical customer status) that goes from a certain time point—let us say seven months—up to the churn window. Some of the data in this data set will be monthly data on consumption, complaints, and so on; other elements of the data typically will be statuses that are the same for the full period, such as gender or geographical location. Then in another data set you compile all the

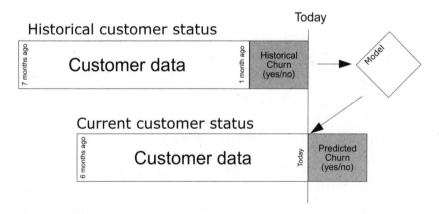

Exhibit 6.4 Time Element of Churn Prediction

churners within the churn window and add them to the historical data set. Since your data set now has information about who churned and who did not, an algorithm can scan through all the input variables looking for which variables, and fields within these variables, discriminate between customers that churned and those that did not. This is how you make your churn prediction model.

The next step is to generate a new data set called "current customer status," which is an updated version of the "historical customer status" data set. Then you allow the model to score your current customer status data set with the trends that it learned from the historical customer status data set. The result is that cases similar to those that churned last month will now be identified and can be handled proactively. The cases can be identified either via a dummy variable scoring high-risk profiles 1 and others 0 or by a variable indicating the risk, as a percentage figure, of customer churn during the next period (equally long to your churn window).

It is rather simple when you think about it. All you say is that if that is how a churner looked last month, it is probably also how a churner will look this month. If you have a market that is relatively stable, you probably can use the same model for a few months at a time; if the market changes constantly, you probably should develop a new model on a monthly basis or more. You should be aware that it typically takes from two to ten weeks to set up a churn prediction model for the first time, but analysts can periodically update the model in a matter of hours, if they are given proper access to data and professional data-mining software. A final and extremely important piece of advice is that you should always make sure that your data mart and the data-mining process is documented. Top analysts are in high demand, and you do not want to start from scratch every time they change jobs.

How the Data-Mining Process Works

The data-mining process is different from traditional statistical procedures. The difference lies in the mentality of the user environment, since data mining often is used in an ever-changing commercial context, based on ever-changing data and data sources. Successful data-mining projects therefore must be able to quickly identify the ever-changing patterns in the data and act on them. In the case of churn prediction, the pattern would be: Which customers are leaving us this month? This is why data-mining algorithms for churn prediction typically can include all variables that potentially could explain why customers churn and automatically select the relevant ones and include them in a model. At times while doing data mining, we will not care so much about whether we can explain exactly the causality between the selected variables and churn; all we want to do is verify that this correlation also can be found when we apply the model to an unknown data set. If you would like to know more about the differences between statistic and data mining, read Chapter 4 in my previous book, *Business Analytics for Managers*, which contains a detailed discussion of the subject.[1]

A typical data-mining process is presented in Exhibit 6.5, which includes getting a historical data set, as shown in Exhibit 6.4. In this more detailed case, the data set is divided into a modeling data set and an evaluation data set. The modeling data set will be used for the modeling procedure also shown in Exhibit 6.4. The difference here is that several models are developed. This can be done using the same algorithm and different parameter settings or it could be done by using different algorithms, such as types of decision trees, neural networks, binary logistical regression analysis, discriminant analysis, and so on.

Depending on the algorithm used and the purpose of the analysis, the modeling data can be split into two data sets, the training data

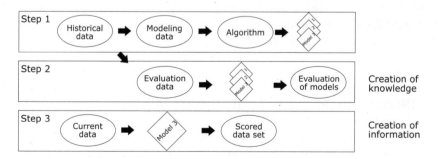

Exhibit 6.5 Modeling Process

and the test data. The algorithm uses the training data to detect patterns; it uses the test data for removing patterns that are only local phenomenon in the training data. The purpose of this procedure is to make models that are general by nature rather than descriptive for a specific data set.

In order to compare the performance of the three models in Exhibit 6.4 they are all used on an evaluation set. An evaluation is a proportion of the historical data set, including the information about who churned, which is set aside to evaluate which of the three models performs best on a data set that they have never interacted with before. The model that performs best here will then be the selected model, if precision is the only selection criteria. Step 3 shows that when a model has been selected, then it is applied to the "current data," which then will generate one or more new fields indicating how similar a given customer is to last month's churning customers on a scale from 0% to 100%, which is interpreted as the chances that this customer will churn during the coming time window. With this information in hand, we know which customers we should approach. On the right side of Exhibit 6.5 it also says "creation of knowledge"; during this point in the process, analysts can sit down and start to interpret the different models, which can give vital input on how the customers should be retained. For example, if it is young customers leaving the company, then we should identify and contact young customers with a relevant message. The bottom right corner in Exhibit 6.4 also says "creation of information"; this means that the output of this procedure is to add one column onto the customer analytical base table that indicates which individual customers are likely to churn. This column could be in the form of a 1 or 0, where 1 would indicate a churn; or it could be a percentage numbers that indicates per customer how likely that customer is to churn in the near future.

FINDING THE MOST VALUABLE CAMPAIGNS

This section was written for processes owners who want to optimize their existing retention activities and have DW information about which customers were contacted when, by which campaign, and

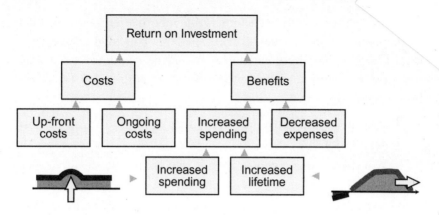

Exhibit 6.6 ROI Tree

whether the customer still is active or not. The aim of this section is to show how you can identify which campaigns are the most valuable for your company from a return on investment (ROI) perspective.

Exhibit 6.6 shows a ROI diagram, which is a visual presentation of the different costs and value drivers that you need to identify to be able to estimate the value of your individual retention activities. This ROI tree is similar to the one presented in Chapter 5 (Exhibit 5.2), where you also can read about how to estimate its individual element costs and benefits in more detail. The difference is that the effects of retention campaigns in regard to the ROI primarily will be manifested through the increased lifetime, which is what this chapter is about, whereas the effect of cross- and up-selling typically can be measured via increased profits or volumes.

IMPROVING THE HIT RATES OF EXISTING CAMPAIGNS

If you have been directed to this section by the decision tree in the beginning of this chapter (Exhibit 6.1), it is because you currently are running retention campaigns yet wish to investigate whether they can become more efficient via targeting only the customer groups where the campaigns have the highest impact. This kind of analysis could be relevant in situations where an organization runs the same retention activities in the same manner over a considerable period of time—for example, follow-up calls to customers one month after they have filed a complaint. From an analytical perspective, you might have concluded earlier that these customers should be contacted since they have a significantly increased propensity of churning. But the questions raised now are:

- Are there some customer types that cannot be saved via this retention call?
- Are there some complaint types that cannot be saved via this retention call?
- Are all service agents equally good at making retention calls?
- If you find some differences, which of the three a's will you go for: abandoning the calls to these customer groups, adapting the way they are contacted, or accepting that this is just the way it is?

Setting Up the Data

The data requirements are covered by the analytical base table as presented in Chapter 5 or the churn mart presented in this chapter. Note that in the specific case of retention calls, it would also be logical to make a churn variable that identifies which customer left in the period between the raised complaint and the retention call; this could provide information regarding whether, in the future, any or the entire set of customers should be contacted earlier.

Selecting an Algorithm and Subsequent Business Process

When choosing an algorithm, you can take one of two paths: You can use an algorithm that you can interpret and, based on whatever knowledge it gives you, you can the update the existing process. If you learn that primarily small customers on short-term contracts still churn despite retention calls, armed with this knowledge, you can reconsider whether to approach these customers differently, earlier, or perhaps with more urgency and with a higher service level in case they are willing to enter on a long-term contract—and if they are worth it. This is, of course, a relatively comprehensive exercise to go through. However, it should be considered for companies in industries with high acquisition costs or those that compete on innovation or have positioned themselves as high-end providers in the industry.

The alternative path is by generating a so-called error correction model, which can identify the customer types that do not respond positively to your retention call anyway and subsequently remove them from the call lists. This means that we go for the abandon option.

IDENTIFYING CUSTOMERS FOR MULTIPLE CAMPAIGNING

If you used the decision tree in the beginning of this chapter (Exhibit 6.1), you were directed to this section because you indicated that you want to start using data mining as input on how you will create your campaigns in the future. This is a relevant approach if you want to improve already existing retention activities in your marketing department, because new data or analytical competencies have become available, or because of a shift in your company toward a retention strategy. There can be many motives for doing multiple campaigning; what is common to them all is their purpose: to improve the way your company does campaigning, which probably also means that you are in the marketing or sales department.

In my experience, the multiple campaigning approach is the single most effective method of all those mentioned in this chapter. It can factually identify what your company should improve and remove all the myths and anecdotes based on case studies and subjective interpretations that otherwise flourish in organizations not used to making decisions based on facts. It can make the customer analytics function a clear voice in your organization since you will become the oracle who can tell on a monthly basis how your company can improve, where the market collapses, and where competition gains market shares from you. Particularly large organizations and market leaders often appear like whales in the water, constantly attacked by smaller and more agile competitors that bite chunks out of the customer base. All the whales can see is the blood in the water. Churn prediction can tell you where the competition bites you and can give you the agility to fight back at once.

From a data perspective, this way of working does not set any new requirements for your analytical base table; however, in terms of algorithms, there are some elements that you should be aware of. Usually when you do data mining, you tend to go for the model that can best predict which customers leave you, when, and why. The analysis is rather simple: Apply your model to a historical data set and see how well it is at predicting which customers actually did leave in the following period. This approach allows for a data-mining process where you can pretty much use any algorithm at hand and pick the one that performs the best. This approach is discussed in the next section, "Identifying Customers for Single Campaigning." In this case, the idea is that we want to identify all available campaigning opportunities and then evaluate on a case-by-case basis whether they have the potential to be launched for real. In other words, we place our customer in a bucket full of holes, and our intention is to identify and close these holes one by one via customized campaigns. As a rule of thumb, two elements must be fulfilled for an opportunity to become a campaign:

1. **You need to be able to isolate a customer need that you can respond to.** In some cases, doing this might be very difficult if there is a market decline for your traditional product. But then again you can consider what your customers demand instead. If you are in the airline industry and you are losing business travelers, perhaps you should consider investing in video conferencing technology since people still have to meet and you might still have a relevant brand. If you are losing customers due to a new strategy, then you can inform the strategy team about the consequences. However, if the intention of the strategy team was to move focus away from this segment, it is usually not a particularly good career move to use your entire marketing budget on retaining these customers.

2. **There should be a sound business case for running the campaign.** The customer segment with a high churn propensity has to have a certain critical mass in terms of size and value. At the same time, the retention activity must be expected to have a certain effect and be within the given budget.

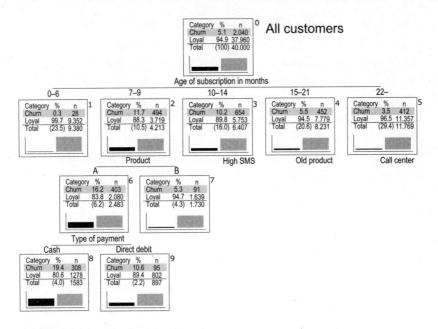

Exhibit 6.7 Interactive Decision Tree

Exhibit 6.7 provides an example of a decision tree used for campaigning in the telecom industry. The specific numbers are representative only, but the trends and the decisions taken are real. A decision tree is built up by a series of nodes starting with the one on top with a "0" to its left, which shows the 40,000 customers that the analysis is based on including the 2,040 customers, representing 5.1% of the total population, that terminated their contract the month before. The model only describes customer-initiated churn; contracts the telecom company churned were excluded from this analysis. From survival analysis and other studies, we know that churn is closely related to the age of the contract. Therefore, the first step in this analysis was to force the model to make its first splits based on contract age. (One contract represents one active telephone number.)

The result showed through node 1 that very few customers terminated their contract during the first six months of the contract, which is not surprising since this would have resulted in penalties. Node 2 showed that in the first few months after termination of the binding period, many customers churned. Essentially these were the customers who signed a contract with the telecom company to get a cheap handset. Since selling a handset would profit only companies like Nokia and Sony Ericsson, not telecom companies that only own the telecom network, some actions were required. Nodes 6 and 7 showed which subscription types could not retain customers and that churn also was closely related to the payment terms. As a result, all customers on product A would be offered product B with a discount if they converted to use direct debit. Similar analysis of node 3 showed that a new kind of subscription was needed for typically younger persons, who used a lot of text messaging as a series of smaller competitors recently started to introduce flat-rate SMS products. This new kind of subscription would be promoted only to relevant users and also would be introduced to the market for acquisition purposes. Node 4 showed that a series of relatively old kinds of subscriptions had become uncompetitive and had to be updated. Node 5 showed that the best explanation for why relatively loyal customers left was related to call center contact. This information was supported by customer interviews that showed that customers often found that the quality of advice offered by a call center agent was not sufficient. In this case (also as shown in Chapter 9), the problem is not something the company could campaign its way out of. It reflected a customer-felt business process that created dissatisfaction (unhappy churn) and had to be fixed.

The result of this decision tree was therefore a series of projects involving product development, customer communication, and the repair of internal work processes. In order to see these opportunities in the data, you should strongly consider inviting your top analysts into marketing strategy and status meetings in order for them to become educated in what decisions need to be taken. In turn, you should expect that a top analyst will be able to educate the sales and marketing team about how information can add opportunities to their plans.

Analysts also should consider using neural networks as support when developing decision trees for two reasons:

1. Based on what the neural networks find to be a good model, you can evaluate whether this manual way of building a decision tree results in a significant loss of precision.

2. Neural networks often come with a sensitivity analysis. This sort of analysis works like a correlation analysis and indicates which of the input variables is good at predicting why customers leave. A sensitivity analysis, therefore, will give you some very strong clues about which variables should have been included—possibly on the top—of your decision tree.

IDENTIFYING CUSTOMERS FOR SINGLE CAMPAIGNING

If you used the decision tree in the beginning of this chapter (Exhibit 6.1), you were directed to this section because you indicated that you want to start a retention campaign using churn prediction. The outcome of this way of doing campaigning is a percentage figure that indicates the risk of every one of your customers leaving within the next month. Based on this figure and the customers value, you can start contacting all the high-risk customers through mail or by phone. Since you will be starting only one campaign, it is assumed that you are interested only in which customers might leave you when, but not so much why, because they are all going to get the same treatment anyway. An example could be if the project is owned by the call center and the essence of the campaign is to call all customers with a high churn risk. It could also be because you work in an organization with low marketing skills that wants to test the value of this customer-centric process. Finally, this way of campaigning can be a very good way of handling customer segments that are too small to be considered for a separate campaign, as described in the previous section. Therefore, it serves as a safety net that ensures that all high-value customers with a high churn risk also get included in a retention program. You can read more about this way of using churn prediction in Chapter 9.

How to Prioritize Customers

The typical way of running such a project is to generate a contact list that on a periodic basis identifies a certain number of customers that should be contacted, possibly only if there is some idle capacity in the call center. You should consider not only the risk of losing a customer but also the value of the customer you contact: the customer's "risk value." Risk value is equal to:

$$\text{Risk of churn} \times \text{Average profit per month}$$

This simple equation can be optimized easily and changed according to your specific business needs, but its core purpose is to handle the trade-off between: Should I call my most valuable customers, or should I call the ones most likely to leave me? By using this equation, a customer you earn $100 per month on with a 10% risk of churning will rank as being equally important to contact as a customer that generates a profit of $20 per month with, however, a 50% risk of churning during the next period since 10% × $100 per month = 50% × $20 per month = $10 risk next month. The logic behind this equation is that if you have a group of customers with a 10% risk of churn within the next month, you should also expect 10% of them to be gone at the end of the next months, including their average earnings. You will not know which individual customers will leave until the end of the month. However, from an aggregated perspective, the logic is valid. For the sake of good order, note that customers should be given a grace period so that you do not contact too often loyal high-value customers that just happen to have a high-risk profile.

As mentioned, this way of prioritizing which customer to contact is simple but efficient. If you have various retention offers (different discounts or gifts), those also should take the value of the customer into account. Chapter 3 explains how to estimate the value of a customer and how to treat customers differently according to value. It also explains how you can implement value-based segmentation organization-wide. Although doing that might be beyond your current project scope, it can be considered as a very serious next project candidate in order to align the high service levels given to high-value customers in your call center with the service they receive across all other customer touch points.

How to Select the Best Model

As emphasized earlier, the primary selection criterion for single campaign models is precision. There are many ways of comparing the

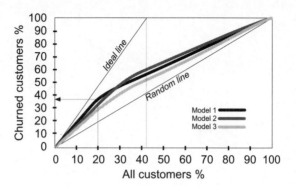

Exhibit 6.8 Lift Chart Comparing Three Models

predictive precision of churn models; one of the most commonly used methods looks like the lift chart presented in Exhibit 6.8. This example compares three different models based on their ability to identify churning customers. The way to evaluate the precision of a model is indicated by an arrow. If you sort your customers based on churn risk allocated to each one by the respective models, using model 1, you will be able to identify 37% of the churners by contacting only the 20% of your customers with the highest churn risk during the coming period. By looking at lines in the lift chart, you can compare the three models. In this case it seems like model 1 outperforms model 2 up to a certain point and model 3 is constantly outperformed. Whether you should use model 1 or 2 is now up to how many customers you will contact, among other things.

Whether this improved hit rate, from 20% to 37%, that you get if you select your customer via the model as opposed to randomly, is a good or a bad result has to do with how close that model curve comes to the ideal line. In Exhibit 6.9, this ideal line indicates that approximately 42% of the customers in the model were churners. Had model 1 been a perfect model, it would have identified all 42% as the ones with the highest churn risk, which also would have resulted in a lift curve equal to the ideal line. The other extreme is the random line, which is how a model with no ability to predict would look in a lift chart. After having scored 50% of customers, a model with no predictive power still would have identified only 50% of the

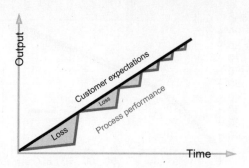

Exhibit 6.9 Improved Responsiveness to Customer Expectations

customers that actually will churn. Thus, nothing is gained from using such a random model.

Standard features of all advanced data-mining software can give you input about how many customers you should contact from a break-even perspective, taking into consideration the cost of making a call, the value of saving a customer, and the predictive precision of the specific model.

Improving the Feedback to Customers

One way that you can improve the quality of loyalty calls to customers is if you include, next to the list of high-risk customers, some indicator variables. An indicator variable provides call center agents with clues about why a customer might be on the verge of terminating his or her contract. If we think about a telecom case, this could be input about whether the customer: has called technical support recently; uses an outdated mobile phone; uses a product that does not really fit his or her calling patterns; and so forth. An indicator variable is generated as an individual model, which based on the handset only predicts whether it provides a churn risk or not. Alternatively the indicator variables can be manually set depending on other business rules. Along with the indicator variables, call center agents can be provided with scripts, training, and retention offers to support their efforts. Obviously not all customers will be on the verge of leaving and not for the reason indicated by the churn indicators, but they still provide

clues to call center agents about what to look for as reasons for customer dissatisfaction.

CREATING SIMPLE WARNING SYSTEMS

If you used the decision tree at the beginning of this chapter (Exhibit
6.1), you were directed to this section because you indicated that you
want to start to use churn prediction and integrate it into your business intelligence systems. By doing this, you can make early warning
systems that inform the relevant staff in case customers have been
exposed to service failures or simply are showing behavior that typically precedes customer churn.

From a process perspective, it is very logical to have the system
contact call center agents or sales reps as soon as a customer shows
increased churn risk. This is opposed to using monthly call lists or the
like; a customer might already have terminated his or her contract by
the time retention calls finally comes around.

This pop-up functionality is standard for DWs, which can push
these warnings out to specific email accounts in customer service or
at the key client manager teams. An example also comes from the
telecom industry, where we set an algorithm to scan the CRM systems
every fifth minute looking for whether any business customers had
made one of a series of inquiries, such as requesting prices for new
mobile phones for its employees or asking for a total review of the
bills they had paid within the last six months. These types of questions
were focused on because churn prediction models had found that
these sorts of requests were strong indicators of churn behavior.
Therefore, the DW would automatically generate an explanatory
email, within five minutes of the event, for the key account manager,
so that immediate action could be taken.

This way of automating the information flow based on events,
known as marketing automation, also can be directed toward customers
and currently is a strong trend within customer intelligence. It is about
automating the interaction with customers in a quick and relevant
fashion. If, for example, a customer registers a new home address, then
the system might send an email to the customer about where the nearest
physical outlet of the company is. If the customer changes the family

name, the system sends a family offer assuming that the customer just has been married. Who knows, one day the automated teller machine might congratulate you on your birthday on behalf of your bank.

What drives the focus on marketing automation is its ability to make cost-efficient and relevant customer communication. Today we might not think much of this trend; however, as analysts improve their ability to predict what is of relevance to customers, as ever-increasing amounts of customer data become available, and as customers get increasingly used to integrating cyberspace into their lifestyle, it is very likely that this phenomenon will become a central competitive parameter in the future. The explosive growth in use of social media may be an early indicator of how willingly we integrate cyberspace into our lives if we find it rewarding.

CREATING COMPLEX INFORMATION AND WARNING SYSTEMS

If you have used the decision tree in the beginning of this chapter (Exhibit 6.1), you have been directed to this section because you have indicated that you want to start using churn prediction and integrating it into your business intelligence systems. To a large extent, what is formulated in this section can be seen as an add-on to what is presented in the last section, where pop-up systems and marketing automation were used to execute churn prevention campaigns. This section also explains how churn prediction or early-warning systems can be implemented for customer scorecards and to set up feedback mechanisms within your organization.

A customer scorecard is a report that sums up what has been delivered to a customer on dimensions that customers believe are relevant, including whether what has been delivered is within the service-level agreements made with the customer. Customer scorecards also ensure a fact-based dialogue and long-term partnership between the two parties.

Feedback mechanism within your organization are necessary to ensure that service-level failures are reported to the responsible parties within your organization while also informing the responsible client manager.

Working with complex warning systems is most relevant in industries that create or deliver complex products or services on a continuous base. It might include a travel agency that on a daily basis provides travel arrangements to large corporations. At first, this might seem like a simple service; however, a client manager for a travel agency has to do a substantial amount of work before he or she can make a customer scorecard for the yearly status meeting that includes, for example:

- How many preliminary bookings has the manager made for a given company within the last months, what was the turn time, and how many of these were converted into actual travels?

- Of the actual bookings, what was the turn time and how many errors happened in the booking process, on a hotel and flight level?

- How many visas and other travel documents were requested, and what was the turn time and error rate?

- What was the price of all the different services, broken down by documentation type, hotels, and flights by continent?

- What was the quality of the issued invoices: were they on time? How long time did it take for the customer to pay bills in "days outstanding"?

- Other things might also be of interest, such as how many complaints the customer has made and how many financial disputes have been raised.

It is relatively simple to set up customer scorecards so that information can be extracted per customer on demand from a DW. This method will enable the customer and the key client manager to manage their relationship via fact-based dialogue rather than arguments based on beliefs.

Churn prediction models also can guide travel agents on acceptable service levels, even if none has been specified by a customer, since a churn prediction model indicates how many service failures typically result in customer churn. Should these negative thresholds be broken, an email can be sent automatically to the responsible client manager, who then must take action. A first action from a client manager would be to request an explanation from the process owner who has failed to deliver; the problem could be many errors in the hotel booking process. The process owner can then find and explain the root cause of the failures, along with when the process will be fixed. Armed with this knowledge, the client manager can contact the customer, who will experience a proactive travel agent who acts on complaints not even filed yet. At the same time, the process owner has been informed that a process bug has to be fixed. In this way customer scorecards and churn prediction integrate the customer perspective deeply into the entire process landscape.

RETENTION AND LOYALTY PROGRAMS BASED ON SURVEYS

If you used the decision tree in the beginning of this chapter (Exhibit 6.1), you were directed to this section because you want to build a loyalty or retention program based on the use of questionnaires. This could be because you do not have relevant (or any) data, or you have decided as a company that there are other benefits from surveying customers. As an example, this survey also can be used as a customer dialogue tool, which implies that customers are given individual feedback by their client managers. It could also be that you plan to use the satisfaction or loyalty scores from your customers as key performance indicators (KPIs) for your organization. In addition, a questionnaire can serve as a process improvement tool that continuously provides the organization and its process owners with feedback about how they are doing in the eyes of the customers.

The advantage of using questionnaire data instead of DW data for loyalty programs is that you can ask customers about whatever you want as opposed to churn prediction, which typically relies on whatever customer-related information you can find in your DW. Such a survey typically is administered periodically to the entire customer base, asking customers about their overall satisfaction with what your company provides and then some specifics, say about the service center, your core product, and your Web site. Such a survey typically has a text field where the customers can specify the reason for the given satisfaction score.

You can use the input from the text fields for individual customer feedback but also to give you a more nuanced picture of what your customers like and dislike about your company. If a significant number of customers complain about the waiting time and the arrogant attitude of your service staff, you pretty much know what to start working with, opposed to a situation where you only know that your average customer satisfaction is 4.6 out of 10.

The problem with working with text fields is that it involves relatively time-consuming analysis that no analysts look forward to doing on a regular basis. When you have or want to collect valuable customer insight, consider using text-mining tools. Text-mining tools provide lists of words that are associated with a specific term when they are placed together in sentences. It could be that the words "call center" are associated with "queue" and "waiting" and that "sales agent" is associated with the word combination "lack of knowledge," "rude," or "unprofessional." This way you can come closer to what causes customer dissatisfaction and can now, based on last month's responses, inform the call center about what process improvements are required.

Exhibit 6.9, which is an elaboration of the process performance concept presented in Chapter 1, shows how rapid, frequent, and precise customer feedback to process owners, in this case created using questionnaires and text-mining, can make a company more responsive to customer needs. The conclusion from this example should not be that "just" because the customers want something, they should get it—it is up to the strategy to decide what you should offer the market. The conclusion is that if there is a mismatch between what customers expect and what you deliver to them, you will have to change either their expectations or your processes or both, since the problem is lack of alignment, and that is what causes customer dissatisfaction and potential customer churn.

One of the most typical problems with loyalty programs is that they often are set up to serve multiple purposes. Instead of becoming master of any, they become average Jacks of all trades. Some examples are presented next.

- If a loyalty program is used as a KPI for sales organization and as a dialogue tool by the salesperson, you will have to decide whether the salesperson should be informed up front about when a customer will be surveyed to ensure the customer responds so that KPIs can be gathered. This will, however, also give the salesperson the opportunity of impacting a KPI, which supposedly should be objective.

■ If client manager and customer dialogue happens once a year, and at the same time you would like to make statistics on call center performance based on the questionnaire, should you ask about performance within the last year, which is most relevant for the dialogue, or performance within the last month, which is most relevant from a call center performance management perspective?

■ If you want to make process performance tracking, you typically want to ask about a specific transaction, since then you can track it down to a system or a person when you need to improve something. However, customer dialogues typically discuss all the transactions that happened across the last period.

■ Should you ask a customer to evaluate the performance of the very salesperson who will give the feedback?

There are many issues to consider before using surveys as the data foundation for running loyalty programs. You might want to consider how many masters your loyalty program realistically can manage at the same time. To read more about questionnaire-based loyalty programs, I suggest that you read the book *Answering the Ultimate Question* by Richard Owen and Laura L. Brooks, which is a follow up on the book *The Ultimate Question: Driving Good Profits and True Growth* by Fred Reichheld, which also gives a good introduction of the subject.[2]

LOYALTY PROGRAMS BASED ON SUBJECT MATTER EXPERT INTERVIEWS

If you used the decision tree in the beginning of this chapter (Exhibit 6.1), you were directed to this section because you want to build a retention or loyalty program and are considering interviewing subject matter experts during this process. Subject matter experts are typically used during the start-up phase of projects which perhaps at a later stage will focus more on using DW data or questionnaires. Another reason could be that you want to learn what it is that drives loyalty rather than churn, where loyalty drivers are the relational elements that positively differentiate what you go to market with, as opposed to churn drivers, which are hygiene factors that differentiate your company negatively if you do not deliver on these basics.

If you are starting up a new churn prediction project, interviews with subject matter experts are natural first steps to help you understand what customer needs are and, based on this information, how to prioritize which data sources should be sourced first and how the data should be presented. This is all described in more detail in the section "Elements Needed for Churn Prediction." These sorts of interviews are also valuable in the early phases of a project to educate the project team and create a shared understanding of terms and priorities.

Retention programs are more than tools that identify and act toward high-risk churners, which is the equivalent of stuffing the holes in a bucket. Loyalty programs also serve as loyalty creators that proactively strengthen the relationship with customers. So where retention programs have an element of fixing the basic customer relations, loyalty programs are about creating long-term competitive advantages by strengthening the customer relations. Where retention programs are about spending resources on retaining dissatisfied customers, loyalty programs are about investing in long-term relations with satisfied customers. When making retention programs, you are looking for what causes dissatisfaction; when making loyalty programs, you are looking for what can improve satisfaction. These different loyalty factors are known either as hygiene factors, which are the basics that simply must be in place, or delight factors, which are unique qualities added by the vendor that positively differentiate a service or product in a market and by so doing creates loyalty. This mind-set is well presented in the book *Blue Ocean Strategy*.[3]

If you are looking for churn drivers, the interview with your subject matter expert typically will start with identifying all the customer-felt processes, such as when people order, buy, complain, or ask for support in relation to what you offer. When you have identified all these customer-felt processes or customer touch points, you then go through them one by one and identify which is a service failure. It might be that the invoice is too hard to understand, too late, too hard to update, too difficult to discuss, or includes incorrect figures. When you have identified the potential service failures per customer touch point, the next step is to go out and identify which ones create the most customer dissatisfaction. One way of identifying what the customers are mostly dissatisfied about can be done by investigating customer complaint logs, interviewing first-line customer support, or surveying or interviewing the customers themselves.

If you are looking more for loyalty drivers, your interviews should focus on customer needs for buying your product. In this case, you are moving away from basic performance management to basic marketing. How these sorts of interviews or workshops can be done is explained in the section "Segmentation Based on Workshops" in Chapter 4.

When you have identified a list of churn and loyalty drivers, you will have to prioritize which one to focus on eliminating or promoting. A good rule of thumb is to start by fixing the basics first, since no customers will be impressed with all your local CSR investments or free movie trips (loyalty drivers) as long as they cannot call in and complain about all the errors that your billing machine makes (churn driver).

SEEING THE RETENTION PROCESS FROM A DYNAMIC PERSPECTIVE

This chapter is about how to use lead information for retention processes and structures according to how your organization is set up to do these processes, as illustrated in Exhibit 6.10. Based on the data you have available, customer analytics will, to a varying extent, be able to create value for your organization. Thus it is important to note that you must invest in data before you can harvest the full benefits from customer analytics. Whether you should invest in customer analytics as a starting point is essentially a strategic question for your organization. Look into your organizational or marketing strategy, and identify whether customer analytics can make your organization meet its strategic objectives. If customer analytics can do so, investigate

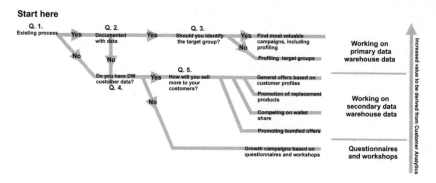

Exhibit 6.10 Improving Your Lead Information for Retention Processes

where in Exhibit 6.10 from a strategic perspective you should be and where you are. Based on the discrepancies that you find, you will get a clear indication about what challenges lie ahead of you.

Chapter 8 provides some tools to enable you to analyze the current customer analytics maturity level of your organization from an overall CRM/marketing process perspective.

NOTES

1. Gert Laursen and Jesper Thorlund, *Business Analytics for Managers: Taking Business Intelligence beyond Reporting* (Hoboken, NJ: John Wiley & Sons, 2010).

2. Richard Owen and Laura L. Brooks, *Answering the Ultimate Question: How Net Promoter Can Transform Your Business* (Hoboken, NJ: John Wiley & Sons, 2008); F. F. Reichheld, *The Ultimate Question: Driving Good Profits and True Growth* (Boston: Harvard Business School Press, 2006).

3. W. C. Kim and R. Mauborgne, *Blue Ocean Strategy: How to Create Uncontested Market Space and Make the Competition Irrelevant* (Boston: Harvard Business School Press, 2006).

CHAPTER 7

Working with Lag Information

What if I told you how all your processes currently are doing and how to optimize them—would that be of interest to you?

Chapters 3 to 6 have presented a long series of data sets, algorithms, and how they can enable improved business processes given competitive and organizational preconditions. This chapter looks deeper into how you can work with lag information, which is how to use process performance information to make decisions of a more operational character during campaign execution.

Most marketers who have launched a campaign have at one point felt: "Now that we have launched the campaign, we can only hope for the best." It does not have to be like this; if you do proper performance tracking, you can abort or adapt the campaign at an early stage if things do not succeed above planned expectations. This is the essence of all performance management and tracking. It is about maintaining the agility of your business processes. Also keep in mind that a campaign can overperform and therefore possibly be rolled out more broadly before your competitors have time to make the expected counterattack after they realize that market share must be regained.

Some old-school sales managers will argue that it is a waste of time to sit and monitor and analyze campaign performance. All the resources that go into analyzing might just as well have been spent on selling even more. This could sound like a good argument to some, but try to imagine a society where no resources are spent on innovation and the risks of failure that inevitably go hand in hand with innovation. If you do, you should imagine a society where everyone still rides in a carriage pulled by horses, yet no doubt in the most efficient manner. The problem is that such old-school sales managers never attempt to innovate their processes to the next level; they never try to work smarter, just harder and harder. Also consider that since this is the information age, your competitors will work smarter and smarter or they will have to move to areas with lower labor costs and work harder and harder there.

STRUCTURE OF THIS CHAPTER

The beginning of this chapter contains a decision tree and instructions about how to use it, as you have seen in previous chapters. This chapter also has a full section on the differences between lead and lag information, since at times the differences between the two concepts can be difficult to grasp. This section could also have been included in Chapter 1, but it serves as a good introduction here. The chapter also discusses the different ways that lag information can create value for you and includes a special section discussing how lag information can create a link between the strategic objectives of your organization and your individual process performance. The rest of the chapter is dedicated to presenting forecasting, the documentation of campaign effects, and the concept of a sales funnel.

This chapter does not have a section on how to do performance tracking of individual processes based on questionnaire data. This would be relevant in only very few situations; for the same reason, the chapter does not include a section on how to get lag information through the use of subject matter experts.

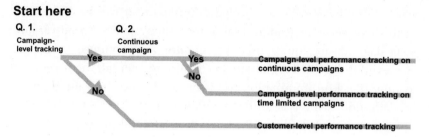

Start here

Q. 1.
Campaign-
level tracking

Q. 2.
Continuous
campaign

Yes — Yes — Campaign-level performance tracking on continuous campaigns

No — Campaign-level performance tracking on time limited campaigns

No — Customer-level performance tracking

Exhibit 7.1 Decision Tree for Evolutionary Process Improvements

LAG INFORMATION FOR EVOLUTIONARY PROCESS IMPROVEMENTS

The decision tree (see Exhibit 7.1) for this section is relatively simply and based on only two questions:

1. **Do you know who accepted the offer on a customer level?** If you do, you will not need to use statistics in order to estimate relationships between cause and effect. You can simply calculate it. Alternatively, as in the case of a radio spot, often you do not know whether a certain customer made a specific purchase as a result of the radio spot or whether this purchase would have happened anyway. In that case, you would say yes to question 1 and use statistics to establish this link between cause and effect.

2. **Do you want to measure the effect of a time-limited campaign, or do you want to optimize an ongoing program based on increased knowledge about cause and effect?**

Before we go to the section on how to use lag information in given situations, we present a general introduction to what lag information is.

RELATIONSHIP BETWEEN LEAD AND LAG INFORMATION

Before we look into a more detailed presentation of how lag information is generated and can be used, first we briefly discuss the relationship between lead and lag information. It can be difficult to distinguish between lead and lag information, and for good reason, since lag information is used to monitor and optimize processes. However, if the process changes become fundamental, then we must assume that lead information has been used, since lead information by definition is the type of decision support used for a fundamental process change. Whether we use lead or lag information, therefore, has nothing to do with what algorithm was used or the type of data but with how fundamental the process change potentially could be for the way you do business. This also means that there might be situations where lead information was produced, but no fundamental changes of the process was created, just minor adjustments. We still would call it lead information because it was created with the purpose of potentially creating a new process.

To confuse things even more, lead information often is created based on thorough analysis of lag information. That is, by analyzing the historical process performance (lag information), we have learned that we should focus only on one product and two segments and abandon the old way of selling (lead information). For example, say your sales budget tells you that you are underperforming with the current number of salespeople; that is lag information. If, based on these numbers, you hire two new sales reps, we still would not call this lead information, even though it is a proactive use of information, because we used the information to do little more than adjust a given process. If, based on sales figures, you concluded that a new sales channel structure was needed and analyzed the earning potential of a web strategy and call center sales force combined with external telemarketing, and then, armed with these figures, made an informed decision about how the company's new sales strategy should look, this would have been a proactive use of information with the potential of revolutionizing the way you sell; therefore, you would have been using lead information.

In many cases it is hard to determine whether changes are revolutionary or evolutionary by their nature. Also, what might be considered revolutionary in a conservative company might be considered a natural process evolution in another company. Typically I suggest that if the change is large enough to require project organization or if the process owner in any way will require additional resources to make the actual change, then it clearly becomes a candidate for a revolutionary change simply because it goes beyond the scope of what the current process is geared to do. This also means that the first time you implement a data-mining model in retention processes, it typically will be a revolutionary change, since it will require new resources coming from outside the existing operational budget. The second model you implement, however, will only be an evolutionary change in the way you do marketing in your organization. What used to be considered revolutionary changes become evolutionary changes over time as processes mature.

WAYS OF USING LAG INFORMATION

The last section discussed the relationship between lead and lag information. The most basic takeaway is that you use lag information to monitor how your current processes are doing and lead information to redesign processes. Lead information often is based on a thorough analysis of lag information. This section looks into the ways that lag information can be used and explains where you can study the subject in more detail. The four reasons we do performance tracking are to:

1. **Monitor output of processes.** The primary purpose of monitoring process output is to make sure that the process meets its defined objectives. This means that lag information must show how a given process performs and at the same time link this performance to the strategic objectives that the process is set to deliver. You can read more about this in the section called "Lag Information as a Link to the Strategic Objectives."

2. **Monitor processes.** Here we do performance tracking so the project or campaign manager can see, on an operational level, how the market activities perform. Besides monitoring the output of the process, as mentioned in reason one, we also continuously monitor what goes into the process, which could

include man-hours, consultancy costs, call center costs, sales-people, and so on. We monitoring processes to improve our target-setting process and learn about cause and effect. You can read more about this in the analytical sections at the end of this chapter.

3. **Become lead information.** To serve as input for process improvement projects in search of new ways to revolutionize the given process. This topic is presented in Chapters 3 through 6 in the cases where the process improvement initiatives were based on data warehouse data.

4. **Become learning information.** Lag information can also be given as input to other sales departments in the rest of the organization to show what they can learn from your processes, and to the strategic department to inform it about strategic opportunities and risks of the current strategy. All this will be explained in greater detail in Chapter 8, which describes how learning information can be managed as a strategic asset.

LAG INFORMATION AS A LINK TO STRATEGIC OBJECTIVES

This book links customer analytics to the company strategy. This linkage becomes particularly strong when it comes to lag information, since its primary purpose is to monitor whether we are about to meet our objectives. As presented in Chapter 2, an organization typically has a strategy (a plan for what it should do within the next year or so). In order for the rest of the organization to execute on this strategy, each department, function, or business process typically is given some objectives (descriptions of what outcome this specific unit is responsible for delivering in order for the overall business strategy to become successful).

Based on these objectives from the organizational strategy, the sales department will make its own sales strategy (again, a plan for how it will achieve its objectives in the coming period). A sales organization typically makes a strategy by selecting and developing the number of campaigns and using the market approach needed in order

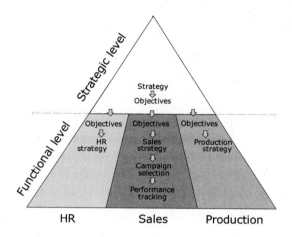

Exhibit 7.2 From Strategy to Performance Tracking

for it to achieve its objectives within its budget and resources. Finally, performance tracking processes are set in order to monitor the success of the chosen sales strategy at any given time within the strategic period (see Exhibit 7.2). Just as the way we do performance tracking has to be aligned with the way we set objectives, the objectives given to the sales department have to be in a measurable format in order for ends to meet. The general rule for objectives is that they be SMART, which is an acronym suggesting that five requirements are fulfilled in order to do effective performance tracking based on organizational objectives:

1. **Specific.** Targets have to be set, such as how many customers you must have by the end of the year, what your revenue must be, by how much you must reduce delivery times, and so forth. Targets that say that your company should be the market leader without defining how this should be measured are not effective.

2. **Measurable.** If it is not measurable, it is not a relevant target. If we do not know how many customers we have, we need to find another target. If it is not possible to allocate revenue and costs to the processes we want to improve, we need to establish some other targets.

3. **Agreed.** The organization must accept the targets. If this is not the case, there is no ownership, and the organization is about to implement a strategy that, at best, will be ignored or, at worst, will be counteracted. It is implicit, too, that accepted targets mean that we have some specific individuals who are directly responsible for the given targets.

4. **Realistic.** Targets must be realistic. I have seen targets accepted without standing a chance of being achieved. This may have something to do with the corporate culture—perhaps someone is trying to buy time or there are no consequences involved in not achieving the targets.

5. **Time-bound.** What is the deadline for reducing sales costs to a certain level and getting 3,000 additional customers? It is also important that we are able, at an early stage, to determine when targets are not being met so we do not waste any more resources on an approach that will fail or add given resources to a process just so that it will succeed. After all, a project without a deadline is just a vision.

LINK TO THE SEGMENT AND TURNOVER MOVEMENT MODEL

If in Chapter 2 you decided to the use the segment and turnover movement model as input for how you will select you future customer relationship management (CRM) activities, it would be a natural next step to measure the performance of these campaigns based on the same framework. To follow up on the example presented in Chapter 2, this would mean that if we set up the four suggested CRM activities, these all should be given individual success criteria and SMART objectives. Also we would expect to follow the overall success tracked via the segment and turnover movement model, since this is the framework that defined to us—via lead information—what we are trying to achieve. Therefore, we need lag information that can tell us whether we are achieving this overall objective or not (see Exhibit 7.3).

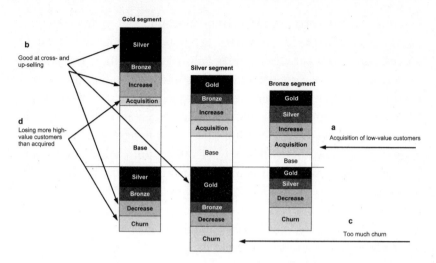

Exhibit 7.3 Analysis of the Segment and Turnover Movement Model

CAMPAIGN-LEVEL PERFORMANCE TRACKING ON CONTINUOUS CAMPAIGNS

If you have used the decision tree in the beginning of this chapter (Exhibit 7.1), you were guided to this section since you want to know about how to set targets and optimize resources spent on campaigns that are executed on a continuous basis. It is a characteristic of these campaigns that you do not know which of your customers (new or existing) received the offer or the market communication. All you have from a data perspective is knowledge about your marketing activities and their effect. The effect could include the number of new customers, additional sales within product categories, and reduced customer churn. In the next example, it will be the number of new customers. This way of tracking sales performance is known to telecom operators, banks, insurance companies, magazines on subscription, and charity organizations with member subscriptions. All these organizations know the number of active customers as opposed to, for example, supermarkets, which typically track the effects as increased sales within product groups.

In this situation, you cannot be quite sure how well your campaigning activities work. If they work extremely well, often you will find that other departments in your organization will try to take credit for these results based on whatever their contribution has been. Success has many parents whereas failure is an orphan. The way to open this black box is to introduce, if possible, campaign codes, which are something that customers report on to gain some sort of a reward. For example, "Enter the promotion code presented in the magazine if you want a special welcoming offer on this new pair of contact lenses." Of course this will make all other "full-paying" customers frustrated since they obviously are missing out on something. The use of promotional codes is something you might be able to do in the future. It provides knowledge on a customer level about the effects of your campaigns as they are executed and will enable you to better set exact targets for future campaigns.

Since you read this section, this is not something you have. You should consider using forecasting models to explain the causes and effects of your sales activities. Learning the causes and effects of your campaigns will give you a lot of knowledge, such as:

- How to configure the most effective campaign given your budget in terms of media mix, effect of different promotions, number of salespeople and their geographical location, and perhaps even their background.

- How to set up targets during campaigns that take time lags into account. The basic question here is: If a radio spot is launched in April, when should you then be able to measure its effect, and for how long will the effect last? It is quite obvious that knowledge about these time lags is important during the campaign, since it will give us an indication about when we can conclude that a campaign is a failure or a success. Therefore, this knowledge provides business agility, since we know when a decision can be made about corrective actions, if needed. The same time lags are relevant if you work through different media and channels at the same time, assuming that there are synergies between television spots and salespeople in the stores, since timing here is of the essence.

- The effect of competitor pricing and promotions on your sales processes and how you can counteract.

From a business perspective, the interesting bit about forecasting models is their ability to detect what matters and what does not matter to your results and at the same time include a time and competitor perspective in your business model. Forecasting models are often presented as a higher science, and they certainly can be made into such. In reality, however, many efficient software packages allow the average controller with basic statistical skills to create a forecasting model, including an interactive market simulator, within a day or two. The analyst or controller does not even have to select which of the many potential algorithms to use; the software typically can pick the best one for the data and include it in the resulting simulation model. If you spend a few days more on the modeling part, the model's precision probably will increase from 85% to 95% of the ultimate model. This ability to simulate, even though the model can be slightly improved, can have a huge impact on how campaigns are done, since the sales manager or the controller now can sit and do simulations of future sales strategies and setups.

As mentioned, there are many forecasting algorithms. From a practical perspective, it very often matters less which one you use as long as it can detect the patterns in the data and make forecasts that are exact enough to be useful from a business perspective. Generally, however, forecasting models look at four elements in the data: time lags, cyclic patterns, one-off changes, and current trends.

Time Lags

First of all, the forecasting model looks at the relationship between whatever you are trying to predict and whatever there is to predict by using time lags. In Exhibit 7.4 you can see an example of how this is done as the data is set up in such a way to show the relationship between "sales" and the "spending on advertising." Not only can you see the relationship between sales and advertising costs in a given month, but you also can see the advertising effect during the following months. If the sales variable therefore only correlates significantly with the month(-1) and the month(-2) variables, this would mean that the forecasting model has learned that the effects of your advertising can be measured only one and two months after it has been on the air.

Exhibit 7.4 Time Lags

Month	Sales	Advertizing	Month (−1)	Month (−2)	Month (−3)	Month (−4)	Month (−5)
200701	1,016	608					
200702	921	451	608				
200703	934	529	451	608			
200704	976	543	529	451	608		
200705	930	525	543	529	451	608	
200706	1,052	549	525	543	529	451	608
200707	1,184	525	549	525	543	529	451
200708	1,089	578	525	549	525	543	529
200709	1,087	609	578	525	549	525	543
200710	1,154	504	609	578	525	549	525
200711	1,33	752	504	609	578	525	549
200712	1,98	613	752	504	609	578	525
200801	2,223	862	613	752	504	609	578
200802	2,203	866	862	613	752	504	609

In the same way, the number of salespeople in your organization could be included in the data, if relevant. Then you could learn about how long it takes for sales force spending to have an effect and what the effect is.

Cyclic Patterns

The second element that forecasting looks for are cyclic patterns, which effectively mean that instead of making a correlation analysis between sales and a time-skewed advertising variable (see Exhibit 7.4), it makes a correlation between sales and a time-skewed sales

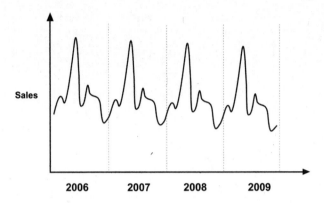

Exhibit 7.5 Cyclic data

variable. In other words, the sale variable will detect whether it correlates with itself. If it does on, let us say, a 12-month basis, then you seem to have a yearly seasonality in your sales. Exhibit 7.5 presents some clearly cyclic data; it could be referring to sales of garden grills in the northern hemisphere, which typically happens in the spring and summer. This sort of information is relevant for some organizations during these seasons. Other business types might find that spending is highest in the beginning of each month, along with the sales on Fridays and Saturdays. In this case, you would probably focus your commercial spots at the end of the week and/or at the beginning of the month, depending on your advertising time lag.

One-Off Changes

Forecasting models can also take bigger changes into account. This could be a merger between two sales organizations that breaks the continuity of your data, a new product version, or a new competitor in the market. The purpose of considering such changes is to maintain the line of data and at the same time estimate the effect of the change (see Exhibit 7.6).

Current Trends

Finally, forecasting models often contain moving averages, which are ways of trying to include data trends that the rest of the model could

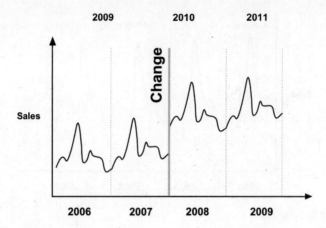

Exhibit 7.6 Illustration of a Change

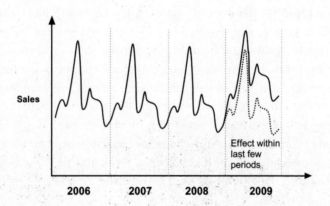

Exhibit 7.7 Systematic Effects over the Last Few Periods

not explain, while at the same time trying to exclude irrelevant variation (noise) in the data. Trends typically encompass only the last few
periods and include the effect of very good weather in the last few
months in our forecast model, since it has an effect on each grill season
that is not expected to spill over to the next season (see Exhibit 7.7).

CONSOLIDATING AND USING THE INPUTS

All the patterns in the data can then be combined into a single forecasting model that, from a graphical perspective, could look like

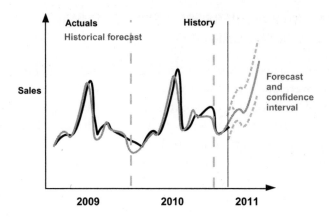

Exhibit 7.8 Graphical Forecast

Exhibit 7.8. There the actual sales are presented in black and the historical and future forecast is presented in gray. Confidence intervals can also be included; they show what the real sales will be in 95 out of 100 scenarios, given that the market conditions known to the model do not change.

The sales manager can now enter the number of salespeople and the advertising costs through whatever media and channels that the model has found to be significant, and see the future effect, including setting up targets by month for the year to come. These targets are essentially what we are trying to meet via the campaigns launched over a year. At the same time, based on the confidence interval, critical limits for campaign performance can be defined that will activate the contingency plans needed for the sales department to meet its targets if corrective actions are needed. Also the model can be continuously updated with market data, which in itself will drive a continuous review on the set targets and new campaigning opportunities and essentially will provide your organization with additional market agility.

Forecasting models are an essential tool in industries with limited space capacity to sell, such as hotels, airlines, and shipping lines, or resources such as call centers, production line capacity, or a limited supply of raw materials. In these cases, the purpose of the forecasting model is also to prevent the organization from overbooking or stretching the scarce resources.

CAMPAIGN-LEVEL PERFORMANCE TRACKING ON TIME-LIMITED CAMPAIGNS

If you used the decision tree in the beginning of this chapter (Exhibit 7.1), you were guided to this section because you want to learn how to set targets and optimize resources spent on campaigns that are not executed on a continuous basis. It is a characteristic of these campaigns that you do not know which of your new customers received the offer or the market communication. All you have from a data perspective is knowledge about your marketing activities and their aggregated effects (e.g., the increased number of customers in your customer base). This is a situation common to telecom operators, banks, insurance companies, magazine subscriptions, or charity organizations with member subscriptions, since they know the number of active customers they service.

Since the lag information presented in Exhibit 7.9 only describes a market intervention that lasted for a month and a half, we will not use forecasting models since they are used for describing long-term relationships between input and output variables. As a rule of thumb, a long-term relationship for forecasting models is three cyclic periods or more, where a period can be defined as years, months, weeks, or days, depending what you are trying to forecast and the data you have available.

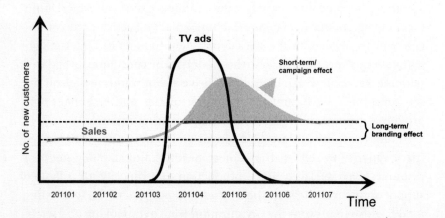

Exhibit 7.9 Effects of a One-Off Campaign

The simplest way to test whether the campaign had an effect is to test whether there is a significant change on a month-to-month basis for the months following the campaign, compared to the average intake of new customers before the campaign. If your customer acquisition process is affected by seasonality, compare your actual customer intake with the forecast or use seasonal correction.

Based on this analysis, you will be able to answer two questions:

1. What is the short-term effect of the campaign, and what should my expectations be of future campaigns?

2. What is the long-term effect of the campaign? (It could be the campaign's branding effect, which also might be something that you should include in the business case and the way you track future campaigns.)

An alternative way of measuring the effect of historical campaigns is to compare them with a similar market or hold-out segment that was not exposed to your acquisition campaign. This way you will not benchmark the effect of your campaign against a forecast or an expected acquisition rate but rather toward customer groups impacted by the same competitor and market conditions as your segment. I have experienced many examples where at first a campaign did not seem to have an effect; however, when the effect was compared to the hold-out sample, which showed a negative market trend, the campaign proved to have helped the company defend its market position.

This way of doing campaign tracking has many similarities with what is presented in Chapters 4 through 6, at the top of the decision trees where the objective was to estimate the return on investment of all your campaigns in order to put more emphasis on the highest-yielding ones.

CUSTOMER-LEVEL PERFORMANCE TRACKING

This section is about how to set targets and optimize resources spent on campaigns that are already being executed or that have been executed in the past. It is a characteristic of these campaigns that you have data on all the prospects that your organization approached and on the result of the sales efforts.

Based on these results, you can make what is known as a sales funnel, which is a model where more goes in than comes out. How you describe the different stages in your sales funnel is up to your selling process and the data that you have available. The sales funnel can be used as an operational tool during the campaign by the campaign managers to monitor how well they are performing. Thus, they will, at an early stage, be able to take corrective action or change the offer or the whole setup. The sales funnel will provide your organization with valuable input on how to set targets for future campaigns. It also will provide your strategy and sales departments with insight on which market segments are relatively easy to penetrate.

The sales funnel presented in Exhibit 7.10 is an example of a telephone sales campaign seeking to acquire new customers. Similar tracking can be done on retention and sales campaigns aimed at the existing customer base. The process is divided into six steps. Since all the steps have different heights, we can at least say that they represent six different elements in the sales process that have the potential to be improved.

1. This step represents a starting point. It is the number of leads purchased by a directory. A directory is a vendor of contact information. Typically we purchase a directory for acquisition

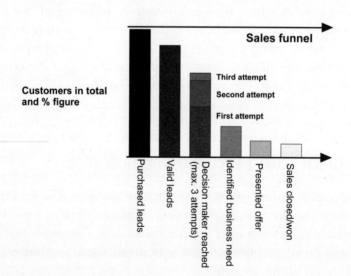

Exhibit 7.10 Sales Funnel

purposes since, according to the nature of the campaign, we will be contacting persons or organizations that we currently are not doing business with and therefore do not have any information about.

2. This step gives a clear indication about the quality of the purchased leads. If this quality issue has to be improved, you will have to look for other providers of this lead information or make a purchase model where you do not pay for invalid leads. At the same time you update contact information for the vendor, bringing value to both parties.

3. This step deals with whether the sales agent reached the decision maker (the person who will decide whether to accept the offer or not). In this example, you can see how many calls it took to reach the decision maker. This is good input regarding how many attempts your sales agents should make (e.g., if there still are relatively many hits on the third call, you might attempt a fourth). Individual sales statistics on sales agents is also relevant in order to identify which individuals or teams to reward or train.

4. This step is a sales agent evaluation. It provides vital input on whether you are contacting the right prospect or whether they simply do not have a business need for whatever it is that you are presenting to them. If there is a large drop here, you might be able to use the same methodology as presented in the section "Profiling Target Groups" in Chapter 4, to improve the way you target customers simply by buying more relevant sales leads and calibrating the offer to match their needs.

5. This step includes all the sales processes where the sales agent was allowed to present the offer that was being promoted in the campaign. In this case there is a very high hit rate, which would indicate that the offer is well designed and presented.

6. Finally, we have the proportion of customers that were converted as a result of this process equal to the hit rate.

Making a sales funnel is a relatively simple exercise. Most of all it has to do with keeping track of things and pulling the information together in a spreadsheet that gives you good insight into what otherwise might have been a black box. A sales funnel will give you insights into whatever steps there are to improve, ranging from data quality, quality of salespeople and target group, and fit of the offer. A tool like this is particularly valuable for large organizations that out-source many telephone-based sales activities. It will enable the organization to monitor the quality of the individual call centers, which can deviate substantially. Merely the fact that workers are being moni-tored often ensures that you get a fair share of their best call center associates to work on your acquisition campaigns. Keep in mind that poor sales agents destroy market value since customers are more likely to say no to your offer the second time that you call them.

CHAPTER 8

Working with Learning Information: The Recipe

Would you like, as a company, to work smarter or would you prefer to continue to work harder?

If you have been reading this book chapter by chapter, by now you should be comfortable with the terms "lead information" and "lag information." This chapter discusses the last information type covered in this book: learning information. The simplest definition of learning information could be that it is lead information on an organizational level. Learning information is therefore feedback to the rest of the organization, making sure that whatever competencies one depart-ment has acquired are used to their fullest extent.

This learning information can be shared horizontally as inter-departmental competency, where interested departments voluntarily reuse what has been learned from customer relationship management

Exhibit 8.1 Vertical and Horizontal Deployment of Learning Information

processes. This knowledge sharing typically is between similar departments, such as other sales or marketing departments working on other industries, promoting other brands, or in other geographical locations. The interdepartmental competency sharing could form a basis of cross-functional joint ventures between, for example, a customer analytics department and the call center and sales department. You can read more about this later in the section called "Using Learning Information in Other Horizontal Departments."

Learning information can also be directed vertically as feedback to the strategy department on a continuous basis, presenting recent learning and new competencies to the strategy team as an input on how successful the current strategy can expect to become (see Exhibit 8.1). This sort of feedback, which goes beyond key performance indicator (KPI) reporting, is a very natural process if customer-centric activities are essential for the overall success of the company strategy. The input could be about whether the current strategy is at risk of failing or whether the customer analytics activities will enable the organization to surpass its current objectives if it becomes even more aggressive in, for example, acquisition and retention. Learning information is therefore also about educating strategic decision makers about the future potential of customer analytics or customer-centric decisions. If strategic decision makers do not see or understand customer analytics as a way of gaining competitive advantages, customer analytics cannot become a strategic asset used in future strategies. In this case, learning information has more to do with educating strategy makers to understand how customer analytics can be used as a competitive enabler. You can read more about the relationship between strategy and maturity of customer analytics in the section called "Using Learning Information to Improve Your Strategy."

USING LEARNING INFORMATION IN OTHER HORIZONTAL DEPARTMENTS

It is a standing joke among strategy consultants that their companies basically all sell the two very same reports to all their customers on organizational strategy: one describing why the customer should start decentralizing its organization and activities and another one describing why the customer should start centralizing. The tricky part for the consultant is to remember which one was sent to the customer the last time and then send the other one this time. There is, however, some logic to this joke, since a very centralized organization tends to become bureaucratized and slow in its response to market changes. For the same reason, the next strategy aims at what we might call "release the creative potential of the organization," and a more decentralized organization is created. Three to five years after the decentralization strategy has been implemented, people tend to find that there is not enough standardization in how the company goes to market, since business units do not communicate well with each other and there are numerous local initiatives that the company as a whole could learn from. The result of these conclusions is that the company will have to centralize and a new strategy, called "building the critical mass to become a market leader" or "making the best initiatives global," is implemented and lasts for three to five years. It might seem like a terrible waste of resources but it also could be seen as a cycle that continuously revitalizes an organization. It can be considered similar to how constant changes between left-wing and right-wing governments keep national politics vibrant and alive in most democratic countries without really changing the absolute fundamentals of these states.

Knowledge management is a tool developed to mitigate the decentralization versus centralization element in large organizations. On one hand it allows organizations to be decentralized and release their creative potential while on the other hand it creates a basis for continuous best practice sharing. The principle behind knowledge management is very simple: The first step is to make a library where, for example, you can upload a summary for each campaign that you launch. The summary could contain information about what you were trying to achieve with the campaign, who the target groups were, who or which roles did what in the campaign buildup and execution, and what the results and learning were. Your local sales department in Ghana can browse through the library and use a campaign executed in northern China last winter for inspiration. In this way Ghana can make a person-to-paper search, but Ghana will also have the opportunity to contact northern China, which means a person-to-person search. This will allow Ghana to talk to a subject matter expert and form a virtual network within the organization. In this way you have achieved a decentralized organization that also makes use of best practices—the best of two worlds—and avoids the enormous costs and momentary loss of market agility that inevitably is part of a radical strategy change.

Often, however, a knowledge management system is not successful, typically because there is little alignment between expectations and what has been promised to users. It takes time to generate such a library. To ensure that all sales organizations use and understand the same format of how a report should be stored, a librarian or knowledge manager is needed. Also it takes time to make a library with content of such a high quality that users come back for more. Just filling the library with low-quality content from a knowledge management competition and/or by asking people just to send in something is counterproductive. Such a knowledge management system, like any other information system, must come with good content, good support, and ease of use, which requires resources. Also, top managers must constantly emphasize and reward the use of this best-practice sharing system.

Even though learning information is defined as lead information on an organizational level, individual departments also will benefit from uploading to knowledge management systems. People do not stay in their jobs forever. It is a huge asset for the next campaign manager to know about how campaigns typically are done, who typically fills in the different roles, and what type of campaigns generally yields the best results.

USING LEARNING INFORMATION TO IMPROVE YOUR STRATEGY

In this section you can read more about different levels of integration between the overall company or sales strategy and customer analytics. The purpose of this analysis is to provide you with a framework to help you analyze how you work with customer analytics today and how you should work with it in the future. There is no right or wrong answer to this; it is essentially down to how your company chooses to compete.

Exhibit 8.2 shows the information wheel (which also was presented in Chapter 1). This exhibit shows how customer analytics can be closely linked to overall company strategy; however, there also should be some feedback mechanisms that provide input on the current and future strategies beyond a KPI level. This exhibit also shows why customer analytics projects so often fail since typically they are cross-functional projects that require strong project manager skills and management support.

Even though there might be many potential stakeholders involved when doing customer analytics, particularly when starting up new projects, the rest of this section focuses only on the relationship

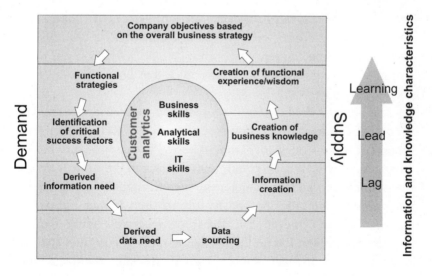

Exhibit 8.2 Information Wheel

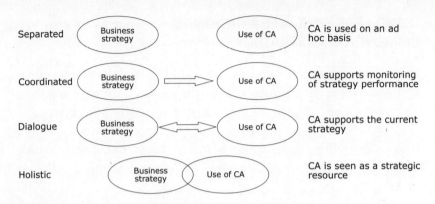

Exhibit 8.3 Relationship between Strategy and Customer Analytics

between the strategy department or whoever is the owner and creator of the strategy-making process and the customer analytics function. This relationship can be well integrated, as shown Exhibit 8.3.

The top layer in Exhibit 8.3 shows customer analytics as being *separated* from how the business strategy is managed. This does not necessarily mean that customer analytics is not used as a means for achieving the objectives set by the strategy. It simply means that within the strategy creation process, there is no reference to the potential and future use of customer analytics. This might not be a strategic mistake; it can be a deliberate and very valid choice made, for example, by a one-person trucking company that has only one customer. As long as there has been a conscious decision not to use customer analytics, it is a strategic choice that potentially can be as good as any other.

A *coordinated* relationship is a situation where customer analytics is used as a strategic lever; however, only from a KPI perspective. In other words the strategy department knows the performance but not what generates it. What is communicated back to the strategy department is only the lag information generated from the customer analytics processes; typically the aim is only to see whether the current strategy will be achieved. This does not necessarily mean that the strategy department has no knowledge about how customer analytics work; currently the focus is just elsewhere, perhaps on implementing other tactical elements of the strategy.

When the relationship with the customer analytics function can be described as a *dialogue*, there is continuously ongoing feedback in regard to the current strategy but not future strategies. This also means that customer analytics are currently only—and potentially rightfully, as long as it is a conscious decision—being used as a tool for solving short-term issues. The dialogue therefore typically concerns whether customer analytics will deliver the expected results.

Since customer analytics is used within the current strategy and it typically involves a lot of sunk costs in information technology and software and perishable expertise among analysts, it is surprising that customer analytics are not used as a means of gaining future competitive advantages. This is typically an indicator that the strategy team does not understand the potential of data and analytics, which is alarming considering that their job is to design how a company must compete in the information age.

In the *holistic* example, customer analytics is used not only as a means of solving short-term strategic issues but also as a means of gaining long-term competitive advantages. This strongly suggests that persons within or close to the strategy team understand and can convey the potential of customer analytics and that they are using these ideas as an active part of the strategy creation process. These people do not necessarily have to belong officially to the strategy team. Perhaps they normally work with customer analytics or are chief information officers who have made it clear how the company can explore and prosper on market opportunities by using customer analytics as a key competence.

At this level of integration between the customer analytics and strategy departments, during the strategy creation process the strategy department will make a thorough analysis of what the last years' most successful campaigns had in common. In this way the department also uses the knowledge management system as a strategic asset that provides information on trends and changes in customer needs and wants. If a customer intelligence department wants to engage further in this dialogue with the strategy team, Chapter 2 presents strategic arguments. You can make a segment and turnover movement model, including some actionable recommendations that can be the starting point of discussions with the strategy team (see Exhibit 8.4). Just keep

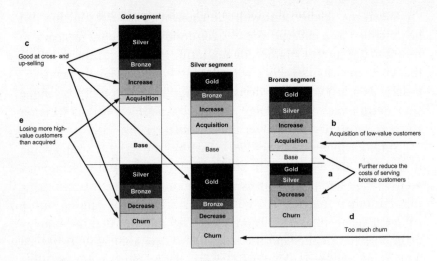

Exhibit 8.4 Analysis of the Segment and Turnover Movement model

in mind that you will be considered like any other functional stake-holder who is trying to promote his or her own interest, so you have to bring some actionable and relevant strategic decision support to the table in order to be listened to.

As mentioned, customer analytics does not necessarily have to be a key component in the way a company competes. If it is not, that omission should, however, be the result of a conscious decision and not the result of lack of knowledge. For many companies and organizations, the use of customer analytics is not a logical choice; however, if your company is competing on strong customer relations and you currently have vast amounts of customer data available, customer analytics may have potential for your organization. To read more about the relationship between competitive value discipline and the need for relevant information system and data repositories, refer to Chapters 3 and 6 in my previous book, *Business Analytics for Managers*.[1]

Another point that must be made here is that customer analytics is not an all-in or no-go question. Customer analytics can be implemented to various degrees, and in principle one degree is not better than the other—that is up to your strategy to decide. What you must be aware of, however, is that it takes time to become an analytical competitor since technical systems and data have to be in place; people have to be trained; and business processes have to be created, changed, and abandoned. In the next section you can see this relationship among systems, people, and processes presented in a maturity model. A customer analytics manager always should have this maturity model in the back of his or her head when discussing the future of customer analytics (i.e., where the company is today, where strategy requires the company to be tomorrow, and how can it get there).

PROCESS MATURITY PERSPECTIVE

This section describes how different technical setups enable you to do customer analytics in different ways. This analysis has to do with the strategic integration of customer analytics with company strategy and recognizing the full potential of customer analytics as a discipline. The aim is to determine whether your current technical setup is sufficient, given your strategic objectives, and to understand what is required to take customer analytics to the next level, given where you are now. As always, there is no right or wrong answer to this; it is essentially about how your company chooses to compete.

Exhibit 8.5 is a maturity model, which is a one-dimensional representation of how customer analytics can be developed over several

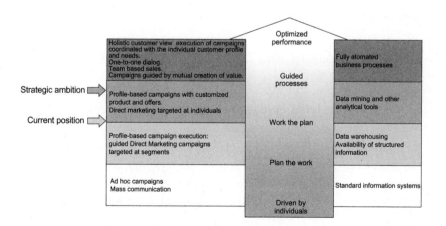

Exhibit 8.5 Maturity Levels, Strategic and Current Position

stages in a given sequence. It is, of course, a crude simplification of a complex reality. One of the main messages of this maturity model is that things have to be done in a logical sequence. What benefit would marketing automation create if you as a company have no idea about latent customer needs that your campaigns are supposed to address? All you would have created is a spamming machine. This simplification can serve as an intuitive framework that both the commercial and the technical side of the organization can relate to. Equally important, it helps you to identify where you are and where you should be from a strategic perspective.

Consider the future potential of customer analytics for your company. If you find it has significant potential of creating more value, then tell key stakeholders or the strategy department and hope for more resources. Also consider whether from a technical perspective you already have been enabled to take your customer analytics processes to the next level. You might already have specialist competencies present within your company; however, perhaps for various reasons a restrictive information technology organization does not allow them to access data. Or you might already have both processes and data in place but no analysts. This case would call for hiring an analyst, educating current analysts, or using consultants.

In the next sections, we describe the four maturity levels in more detail from a commercial, technical, and data perspective. As always, the big question is: Where are we today, where should we be tomorrow, and how do we get there?

Ad Hoc Campaigns and Mass Communication

Ad hoc campaigns and mass communication (see Exhibit 8.6) is the lowest maturity level described in the model. Campaigns on this level are based on data extracted directly from data sources, which give low data quality used for mass communication. Generally lack of managerial awareness of the potential of customer analytics or information management is matched by equally few skills on an operational level. Campaigns typically are generated by individuals on an ad hoc basis.

Exhibit 8.6 Ad Hoc Campaigns and Mass Communication

Profile-Based Campaign Execution

Profile-based campaign execution (see Exhibit 8.7) is the second lowest maturity level, where campaigns are guided toward target groups based on common business logics, and input based on customer surveys is described. Technical business intelligence competences are present in the organization and the data quality is improving. There are few or no analytical competencies present in the organization; the main objective of the data warehouse is to create reporting. The marketing department works with targeted marketing in a more or less structured and planned manner and with limited or no

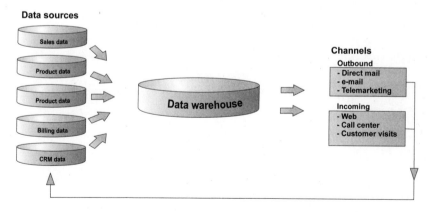

Exhibit 8.7 Profile-Based Campaign Execution

attention from top management. New campaigns are generated based on beliefs and ideas of individuals; only to a minor extent are they backed up with data.

Profile-Based Campaigns with Customized Products and Offers

Profile-based campaigns with customized products and offers (see Exhibit 8.8) are the second highest level in the maturity model. Customer analytics on this maturity level is seen as an important and integrated way marketing is done and has top stakeholder support. Analytical competencies and software are present in the commercial side of the organization or in commercially oriented business intelligence competence centers. Both lead and lag information is created in order to look for ideas for new campaigns as well as to monitor and optimize existing ones. The quality of the analytical work is to a large extent dependent on the individual skills of the analysts. Campaigns are targeted on a segment level on a batch or monthly level. If you would like to read more about business intelligence competence

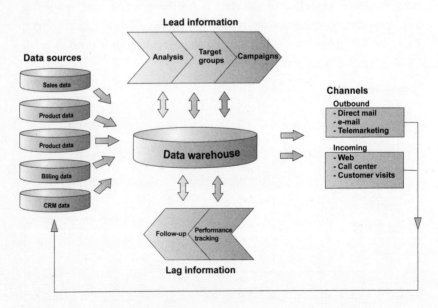

Exhibit 8.8 Profile-Based Campaigns with Customized Product and Offers

centers, what they do, and how they should be organized, see Chapter 7 of my previous book, *Business Analytics for Managers*.

Holistic Customer View and Marketing Automation

Holistic customer view and marketing automation (see Exhibit 8.9) is the highest maturity level in the model. Campaigns are executed based on the principle of marketing automation, which means that they get executed on a one-to-one level triggered immediately and with no human intervention based on changes of customer status in the data warehouse or campaign response from the customer. It could be a change in address that generates mail with information about the nearest outlet to the new address, or a change in surname which triggers a customer dialogue uncovering whether the customer should get a family offer or an offer for singles. Offers provided across channels support each other, and the analytical focus is based on continuously monitoring and updating the performance of the many campaigns running at the same time and being executed to customers (the top right corners of the decision trees in Chapters 4 through 6). The technical focus of the process is to create seamless integration

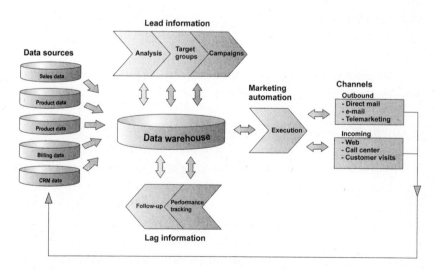

Exhibit 8.9 Holistic Customer View and Marketing Automation

between channels and information systems. Customer analytics and marketing is seen as a strategic resource and continuously supported by top management.

Based on this maturity analysis, you can determine where you are as an organization today in regard to customer analytics and where your company strategy requires you to be. This analysis might lead you to consider whether your organization understands customer analytics and has the ability to make a conscious decision about how intensively it should be used. It also can trigger some reflections about whether you and your analytical team understand and can describe the potential customer analytics offers, since it essentially is you who should sell it to the rest of the organization. The maturity model should give you a clear indication of the sequence of how your customer analytics-driven marketing processes must be developed, since you will not be successful in generating lead and lag information for one-to-one marketing without a data warehouse, and you will not be successful in marketing automation if you have no data-mining models on which to base your communication.

In some cases you might find that what blocks an increased focus on customer analytics is the organizational culture; in this case, you probably are up against the mightiest enemy of them all. As strategists say, "Culture eats strategy for breakfast." Even if you get customer analytics on the strategic agenda, the rest of the organization may not support your efforts, and then you are doomed to fail. This sort of culture can come from many places, but very often it has been fueled by a long series of failed data warehouse projects, poor data quality, and amateurs promoting customer analytics without being able to deliver anything.

In such a situation, you should not focus on a full rollout but generate a series of small and concrete successes to build up credibility and momentum among selected stakeholders. When people in general are more afraid of not being a part of your projects than participating in them, you will have won. You can read more about this in the book *Competing on Analytics*.[2] You can also visit www.basm-support.com and download my executive MBA dissertation which also discusses this subject. Since it also deals with stakeholder management, you can also read Chapter 3.

NOTES

1. Gert Laursen and Jesper Thorlund, *Business Analytics for Managers: Taking Business Intelligence beyond Reporting* (Hoboken, NJ: John Wiley & Sons, 2010).

2. Thomas H. Davenport and Jeanne G. Harris, *Competing on Analytics: The New Science of Winning* (Boston: Harvard Business School Press, 2007).

CHAPTER 9

Case Study of a Retention Strategy

The purpose of presenting this case study is to show how customer analytics looks when it is being implemented for real. The purpose of this chapter is to make it clear that customer analytics really is less about using the most advanced algorithms and optimized technical solutions and more about coming up with some effective and efficient ways of dealing with your customer-centric challenges, which very often can be quite the opposite.

I considered making this chapter the first one in the book, as I always start with this case study when I train classes in statistics, data-mining, and the use of software. Since this case study shows the power of customer analytics, it can turn a company around in a matter of months.

In 2004, a Danish telecom provider realized a loss of approximately $10 million in a market with declining rates. This loss had also resulted in changes in the top leadership structure, and the company had also just been sold to a new foreign company owner. In the summer of 2004, another redundancy round was announced along with another change of chief executive officers (CEOs).

Behind all these numbers were some very high churn figures. In one month the company had lost approximately 14% of its private mobile postpaid customers due to a poorly planned rate increase forced through by the previous company owners. In general, however, the churn levels were between 5% and 7% per month in 2003 and 2004. The new owner of the company introduced an objective to the sales and marketing department dictating that the churn rate per month should be reduced to 2% from the beginning of 2005.

MAKING A TEAM

A customer relationship management (CRM) team was formed to solve this task. The team members included:

- A representative from the strategy and decision support department to be responsible for customer analytics (me)
- A product manager, who would create the retention products
- A communication manager, who would promote the changes
- A representative from customer service, who to a large extent would drive the changes
- Top management, the CEO (to secure focus on the project), and the head of sales and marketing

Some requirements to the overall earnings per customer were also defined. However, short-term focus would be on reducing the churn.

PROGRAM-LEVEL LEAD INFORMATION

The team was finally formed in September 2004. It identified as its first task the collection of lead information about the different kinds of churn that the company experienced. This was chosen as the first focus because it became apparent that customers left for various reasons, that is, there were many kinds of churn.

First of all, the telecom provider itself churned customers who did not pay their bills. Second, customers churned themselves. Customers could churn if they had received a better offer from a competitor or

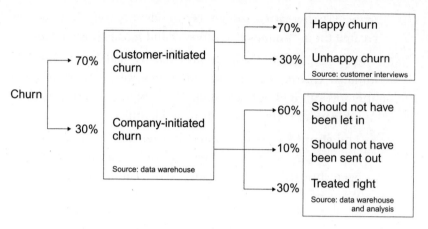

Exhibit 9.1 Lead Information that Defined Subsequent Initiatives

if they were dissatisfied with the treatment they had received from the company.

Analysis revealed that there were even more kinds of churn. Exhibit 9.1 presents the ways customers could leave the company in a mutually exclusive and covering manner. The different churn types will be presented in more detail in the paragraphs to come. As mentioned, there were two kinds of churn: company-initiated churn and customer-initiated churn. Based on data warehouse information, this split was found to be 30–70:

- Focusing on the customer-imitated churn, based on interviews with customers who had churned, it was estimated, that 70% of these customers overall were satisfied with the treatment they had received from the company; they simply had received a better offer from a competitor. To stop this sort of churn, we had to develop a way to give the right customers the right offer at the right time. Hence churn prediction would become what generated the lead information needed to target these "happy" customers.

- Customer interviews also revealed that 30% of customers left the company because they were dissatisfied with treatment they had received from the organization. The lead information required, therefore, should be to identify which processes created these "unhappy" customers and repair those processes.

■ The initial analysis also indicated that we had 30% company-initiated churn, that is, customers who after three dunning attempts still had not paid their bills. Three different processes to mitigate this kind of churn were identified:

1. **The should-not-have-been-in segment.** Sixty percent of the company-initiated churners were customers who had been churned by the company before with no debt recovery. We needed to ensure that our acquisition processes did not allow for these sort of old acquaintances to become customers again before they had cleared all their old debt.

2. **The should-not-have-been-out segment.** Another category accounting for 10% of the company-initiated churn was identified as "old and stable" customers who, contrary to their historical behavior, had ended up in a dunning process. We planned to send these customer an SMS saying that if they started to pay via direct debit services within a month, the dunning fee would be deleted. We also would explain that they would never be subject to a dunning procedure again.

3. **The treated-right segment accounted for 30% of the company-initiated churn.** This segment contained none of the old acquaintances but had to be churned because they were either not willing or were not able to pay their bills.

From an overall perspective five project candidates had now been identified based on the lead information presented in Exhibit 9.1. These projects were the cornerstones of the turnaround program and will be described in more detail, except for the should-not-have-been-out program, which was never realized (see Exhibit 9.2). We had now identified the holes in the bucket and were about to close them one by one.

From a customer analytics perspective, we had created the overall lead information for the turnaround program. Now we needed to generate the lead information for all the individual projects.

Exhibit 9.2 Description of the Program from an Information Management Perspective

HAPPY CHURN PROJECT

The project that received the highest priority was called the happy churn project, as it in fact exhibited one of the telecom company's biggest problems: an outdated product portfolio, which had not been adjusted along with the development of the mobile market.

As shown in the lead information presented in Exhibit 9.1, about half of all customers who left the company fell in the category of happy churn. These were customers who were happy enough with the company but merely had received a better offer. Should such churners be maintained, it would be a question of contacting them at the right time with the right offer. This kind of knowledge can be generated through a churn prediction model, which is a statistical model that, based on the customers who left the company during the last period, can create a profile of them based on data warehouse information. We could then interpret this profile as an independent analysis that gives input about why we were losing in the market. Furthermore, we could assume that next month will be like the last, which means that the profile can be used for scoring all existing customers. Based on this, we knew on a one-to-one basis whom to contact with what retention offer based on how likely the individual customer was to churn and why.

Exhibit 9.3 shows a tree structure that groups customers by their churn indicators. Based on this model, we could describe the overall approach the company should follow. The figures in the model are masked but show the correct trends. It is also worth noting that this model is based only on customer-initiated churn.

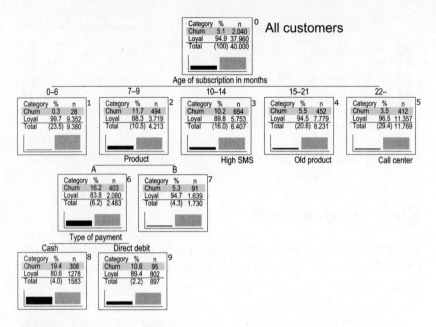

Exhibit 9.3 Churn Prediction Tree

The churn prediction tree, which was based on a so called CHAID algorithm, consisted of 10 nodes, as shown in Exhibit 9.3. Node 0 indicates that 40,000 subscriptions went into the analysis and that 2,040 of these had churned during the last month, equivalent to a churn rate of 5.1%. This data-mining technique is based on letting the algorithm determine which variable in the data set best explains churn, including how data should be categorized within the variables (zero to six months, etc.). Analyst can overrule the algorithm, if necessary.

The algorithm found, as shown with nodes 1 to 5, that the variable could best explain churn via the age of the subscription; there almost was no churn within the first six months of subscription lifetime—the binding period—when canceling a subscription would be very costly for customers. In months seven to nine, there was an increase in the level of customer-initiated terminations, bringing it up to 11.7% for this period. When we drilled deeper into this group, the algorithm found that there were different churn levels between the products.

The subscription types that fell into the high-risk group (node 6) all included a fixed amount payable each month regardless of consumption, even after the binding period had ended. The products that did not include a fixed subscription element had a significantly lower churn rate. When we broke node 6 down further, we discovered that customers who received monthly statements had a churn rate near 20%.

To counter what we found in nodes 6 to 9, we created a subscription where if the client had direct debit, then he or she should not pay a fixed month subscription fee. This new retention product had four benefits:

1. Customers who used the direct debit product would integrate this subscription type in their daily lives. In contrast people who receive a bill in the mail every month are constantly reminded by the bill that they talk a lot on the phone and that they might be able to save money by switching to another telecommunications company.

2. Customers who receive a bill once per month are constantly reminded to pay money, otherwise they will be punished. If they stop receiving bills in the mail, because they are paying by a direct debit product, letters from the company in the future suddenly go from being a negative experience (a bill) for them to potentially becoming a positive, which should be seen as an important part in creating a loyalty program.

3. Other benefits of getting customers into using direct debit services were that in general, in order to use the service their banks should accept this, which in turn meant the product did appeal less to some of people with the worst payment behavior in the market. Avoiding these people would ultimately reduce company-initiated churn.

4. If customers go through the trouble of enrolling the subscription into their direct debit account, we would also expect that they intended to engage in a longer-term relationship with the company.

Based on our research, we had to establish a new subscription type, where customers with direct debit paid no fixed amount each month and customers who did not enroll in direct debit had a fixed amount added to the subscription fee. Since mobile companies typically subsidize new mobile phones for their customers, during the binding period a fixed amount will be required as a part of the subscription to pay for the handset. Therefore, a campaign should also be created reminding clients that they should not pay the fixed subscription anymore when they exited the binding period.

Campaigns should also be created aimed at customers who had some of the "old" subscriptions, since they now could get a new and cheaper one. It may not sound like a good business idea to give customers the same subscription as before but cheaper. But from customer lifetime perspective, it means that customers would be there substantially longer. All of a sudden, it would make very good business sense. Also, it is usually better to cannibalize your customer base than it is to lose the base entirely.

When we dug deeper into node 3, we found that many customers who left were young, heavy users of SMS. We had to gear retention products to them, which we did by offering a fixed price per month for unlimited texting.

Generally we could say about the subscriptions typical among the churners in node 4 that they were "old" and therefore relatively expensive in a telecommunications market that over the past few years had witnessed an intensified price war. The old subscription types therefore were also included in the payment service campaign.

Finally, we found that an old subscription, which typically had been updated once or twice over time, typically terminated the contract in connection with contacting customer service. This issue also gave rise to a separate project, which is discussed in the next section.

So far we had used the churn prediction model only to identify segments in the customer base, which was so large that it had the critical mass required to make it economically profitable to run independent campaigns against the segments. But around the customer base, there were many small segments that also had a lot of churn.

We handled these by another type of churn prediction model, one based on neural networks or whatever algorithm performed the best.

All customers who did not fall into some of the critical segments identified by the churn prediction tree in Exhibit 9.3 still could become candidates for retention activities. These customers would get assigned with a churn risk score between 0 and 100, which described the likelihood that they would leave the company during the next 30 days. This risk figure was then multiplied with the average revenue per customer, which would indicate their risk value. Finally, the 5,000 customers with the highest risk values would be contacted by the company on a monthly basis. These call activities ensured that the most valuable customers always would be given the proper attention.

Lag information that could measure the effect of the specific project was produced for the happy churn project as well as all the others. This was a relatively simple task since we knew how much churn there currently was in each of the segments that we approached and had made some assumptions about how much the churn-reducing effects should be per campaign in order for the program to be successful. We could enter these two sets of information combined into a single report, which showed whether the individual campaigning activities lived up to their expectations. Since the team met weekly, the reporting should also be weekly.

Exhibit 9.4 shows how the lag information for four of the campaigns looked (however, not with the original figures). It was a part of the overall reporting that tracked how close we were at getting down to the 2% churn a month across the full program. The table produced showed for each target segment both customer-initiated churn and company-initiated churn (and the combined amount) and whether this churn figure was above or below the campaign target (a minus would indicate too much churn). Since customers would be bound for an additional four weeks after canceling their subscription, we would be able to forecast some weeks ahead of the gray column (week 48), which was the current week. This way we would be able to see which campaigns performed above and below expectations and roll them out further or maintain, adapt, or cancel them.

Exhibit 9.4 Lag Information for the Campaign Elements

		2004														
		10					11					12				
		40	41	42	43	44	45	46	47	48	49	49	50	51	52	53
Conversion old prod.	Cus. Churn	11	43	39	50	46	39	45	32	49	7	37	38	28		
	Comp. Churn	5	22	19	25	23	20	22	16	25						
	Churn	16	65	58	75	69	59	67	48	74	10	56	57	42		
	Target		−5	2	−15	−9	1	−7	12	−14						
Conversion spec. prod.	Cus. Churn	3	63	56	57	63	57	50	56	64	13	50	57	43		
	Comp. Churn	2	32	28	28	32	28	25	28	32						
	Churn	5	95	84	85	95	85	75	84	96	20	75	85	64		
	Target	5	−5	6	5	−5	5	15	6	−6						

Payment campaign	Cus. Churn	12	41	49	50	39	41	45	56	38	8	50	51	57
	Comp. Churn	6	20	25	25	19	21	22	28	19				
	Churn	18	61	74	75	58	62	67	84	57	12	75	77	86
	Target		−1	−14	−15	2	−2	−7	−24	3				
Churn prediction using neural networks	Cus. Churn	8	13	1	53	48	6	6	12	27	18	34	37	25
	Comp. Churn	4	7	1	27	24	3	3	6	14	27	51	55	38
	Churn	12	20	2	80	72	9	9	18	41	27	51	55	38
	Target		40	58	−20	−12	51	51	42	19				
Total	Cus. Churn	38	164	154	204	241	184	142	174	198	15	155	164	154
	Comp. Churn	13	77	64	111	53	31	76	24	70				
	Churn	51	241	218	315	294	215	218	198	268	15	155	164	154
	Target	2	19	42	−55	−34	45	42	62	−8				

UNHAPPY CHURN PROJECT

Unhappy churn was defined as those customers who had churned because they had been dissatisfied with the service or treatment they had received. As mentioned, here we wanted to identify and fix the processes that pushed the customers away. We had obtained knowledge about customers' dissatisfaction through monthly interviews with some clients who were in their notice period.

One of the big churn drivers (something that pushes customers away) was that customers told us they had to call in to customer service several times to get a problem solved. Independent of this, the churn prediction model also demonstrated a link between the people who used the call center and those who later terminated their subscriptions (node 5 in Exhibit 9.3).

Customer service independently also contacted the churn team to get access to some analytical skills. The department's challenge was also to minimize the number of customers calling in several times in order to free up internal resources, which effectively would be the same as minimizing the number of customers who were annoyed with the quality of the customer service center. In this situation we defined a "recall" as having occurred if the same customer called in for the second time with the same problem within a week, since we would assume that the problem was not solved first time around. Solving problems the first time would mean large financial savings for the customer service center; for the CRM team, the benefit would come from minimizing a churn driver.

From CRM systems, we could see which phones numbers had called in on what date. We could also identify the agent who had handled the problem and the nature of the problem, which could be anything from setting up GPRS to terminating a landline connection. If we found that the same phone number had been registered twice in a week calling in with the same problem, we would assume that the agent who had handled the first call had not solved the problem. This first call would therefore get a mark in the customer analytics solution.

Based on this simple data procedure, a wide range of possibilities were developed. Since we could (as shown in Exhibit 9.5) identify

Exhibit 9.5 Critical Call Types for General Educational Plans

		2004											
		October						November					
		40	41	42	43	44	Total	45	46	47	48	49	Total
Fixed net	Internet	59	42	89	57	41	288	57	54	26	59	54	250
	Fax	12	26	24	15	25	102	23	25	41	21	21	131
	Speech	215	186	247	122	157	927	251	241	186	115	241	1034
	General	351	352	268	351	215	1537	354	143	298	233	265	1293
Mobile	WAP	23	36	24	25	21	129	35	21	24	36	21	137
	MMS	12	16	14	15	13	70	15	18	12	16	11	72
	Email	45	34	12	46	48	185	41	36	35	31	22	165
	Setup	54	25	59	45	75	258	61	62	42	45	51	261
Credit	Dunning	211	255	233	195	300	1194	241	266	184	201	211	1103
	Errors	15	12	550	254	81	912	45	21	26	25	15	132
	OCC	1	22	9	8	2	42	8	4	5	6	1	24
	General	152	142	161	124	152	731	133	131	142	150	111	667

which types of incoming calls the agents had problems solving, we could organize their training accordingly.

The information could also be used on an agent level where we could count all recalls per month and divide it by the number of incoming calls each agent had received. We could then convert this ratio, called the recall rate, into an index, ranging from zero to 200 (average 100) and use it as a quality measure. In this context, "quality" was defined as the ability to solve customers' problems. Since we also knew how many incoming calls each agent had taken, it was also possible to create a quantity index. Similarly, "quantity" would be defined as how many incoming calls each agent answered in a day. These two figures together could provide input to a bonus system, as shown in Exhibit 9.6.

Agents who wanted to increase their bonus could see where there might be room for improvement (e.g., taking more calls or within which categories they generated recalls). Likewise, team leaders would also be assessed by how they were able to educate and motivate their group via an assessment tool as shown in Exhibit 9.7.

The tool is based on putting the quality and quantity indexes up against each other. Exhibit 9.7 shows an example where there are agents in all the quadrants.

- Agent E has a good ability to solve problems but for some reason is not taking many incoming calls. Here, a conversation about what it takes to motivate the agent may be appropriate.
- Agents A and C take many calls but also generate many recalls. In this case, education would probably be appropriate.
- If start-up problems are not what place agent B in the crisis quadrant, the results might suggest that the agent possibly cannot or will not work in a call center, which is something that a team leader should respond to.
- Agent D, who is in all ways doing well, could perhaps be used to lift the rest of the team.

The lead information that was needed to initiate this process improvement was provided primarily by the call center. We did have some information indicating that there was a problem, but the

Exhibit 9.6 Bonus System for Sales Agents

| | | 2004 | | | | | | | | | | | | Bonus | | | |
| | | October | | | | | | November | | | | | | | | | |
Team	Agent	40	41	42	43	44	Total	45	46	47	48	49	Total	Quality index	No. of calls	Quantity index	Bonus score
Team 1	Agent 1	0	1	5	1	0	7	2	1	4	1	2	10	200	350	136	168
	Agent 2						0	0	0	1	0	1	1	3	200	57	22
	Agent 3	5	4	11	11	5	36	20	21	14	11	20	86	31	314	122	77
	Agent 4	2	4	5	7	8	26	5	1	6	7	2	24	111	87	34	72
Team 2	Agent 1	12	-	11	2	4	29	4	5	4	7	2	22	121	541	211	166
	Agent 2	0	0	1	0	2	3	1	2	2	0	0	5	200	54	34	117
	Agent 3	5	4	7	7	1	24	2		2	4	8	16	166	374	148	156
	Agent 4	11	15	12	22	22	82	12	21	26	23	33	115	23	421	164	94
Team 3	Agent 1	1	2	1	1	3	8	1	4	1	2	0	8	200	24	97	148
	Agent 2	8	7	4	9	5	33	4	4	5	7	1	21	126	320	125	126
	Agent 3	1	22	9	8	2	42	8		5	6	1	24	111	123	48	79
	Agent 4	2	4	1	1	1	9			2	1	1	4	200	157	61	131

Exhibit 9.7 Team Assessment Tool

practical knowledge about the process and how it could be improved was identified through interviews with senior call center executives. When the tools were handed over to the process owners they would be able to report on the reduced number of recalls, which would indicate their savings. The CRM team knew the trend over time and therefore could also statistically measure whether the call center-generated churn had declined.

SHOULD NOT HAVE BEEN IN PROJECT

The project on customers who should not have been customers was very quickly given a high priority. Based on program lead information, we could see that there were huge problems with the way we credit-checked our customers. For example, we found that one man, named Ibrahim, on day number 149 of the year had already been churned 147 times the same year. After some reflection, we did not name the project after him. But here was a man who went out almost once a day, bought a phone for less than $100, and sold it and the SIM card for a personal profit, without ever paying the company. The telecom company at the same time, once a day, chose not to go after the person since it was a relatively small amount in play, and since this person did not have the money anyway. However, the company did not recognize that the same person continuously came back and, under the radar, pulled the same trick. Every time Ibrahim did his trick it

Exhibit 9.8 Simple Report that Showed the Problem

Address	City	Account	Name	Loss	Agg Loss	Count	Gross	Churn
Street 12	Town	95944478	name1	5278	6677	7	01-02-2005	31-05-2005
Street 12	Town	95944478	name1	5278	6677	7	01-02-2005	31-05-2005
Street 12	Town	95944478	name1	5278	6677	7	03-03-2005	31-05-2005
Street 12	Town	98654875	name2	554	6677	7	08-08-2004	05-03-2005
Street 12	Town	98654875	name2	554	6677	7	08-08-2004	05-03-2005
Street 12	Town	98654875	name2	554	6677	7	09-10-2004	05-03-2005
Street 12	Town	45864211	name1	845	6677	7	09-10-2004	02-02-2004
Road 3	Village	56456312	name1	1154	4452	6	03-03-2001	06-05-2005

would cost the company between $600 and $800 in subsidies to the outlet that sold the phone, subsidies for the telephone, usage of outside networks accessed via the SIM card, and internal processes. And there were quite a lot of Ibrahim's out there; the trick had become popular.

Since names can be spelled in many ways, we found that searches on an address level provided a better outcome. Exhibit 9.8 shows how the lead information for this program was set up. In this example, you can see from the list that there have been seven terminations of subscriptions on three accounts set up in two different names.

This lead information was really quite simple, because it was a table with all the customers who had been churned during the last month, how many times they had been previously terminated, and a summation that told something about the financial losses over time.

In principle, the lag information on project level was the same. The project goal was to make sure that those persons who had already left the company without paying their bills should not have the ability to become customers again before settling the old debt. This list also could be used to monitor whether the activities had an effect. For any new cases, we could search back in the acquisition process to find out what went wrong and close the hole.

TREATED-RIGHT PROJECT

The treated-right churn category consisted of first-time customers who never paid their bills but bought a subscription to get a free mobile phone and a SIM card. Since these were first-time customers, of course the company had no history on them in the data warehouse and therefore it could not have prevented them from getting their first mobile phone and SIM card. Therefore, they should also be treated based on their actions, meaning that they should be given a subscription and that their subscription should be closed down and sent to the bill collector.

In this context, we made some general rules for how much customers could owe without indicating in any way their willingness or ability to pay their bills. For example, we put limits on how much customers could call for and how many mobile phones customers could obtain before the first bill was paid.

The lead information was the same as for the should-not-have-been-in project, where the focus here was on cases where no bill was paid and there was only one terminated account (see Exhibit 9.9).

Exhibit 9.9 Part of the Lead Information

Address	City	Account	Name	Loss	Agg Loss	Count	Gross	Churn
Street 12	Town	95944478	name1	5278	6677	7	01-02-2005	31-05-2005
Street 12	Town	95944478	name1	5278	6677	7	01-02-2005	31-05-2005
Street 12	Town	95944478	name1	5278	6677	7	03-03-2005	31-05-2005
Street 12	Town	98654875	name2	554	6677	7	08-08-2004	05-03-2005
Street 12	Town	98654875	name2	554	6677	7	08-08-2004	05-03-2005
Street 12	Town	98654875	name2	554	6677	7	09-10-2004	05-03-2005
Street 12	Town	45864211	name1	845	6677	7	09-10-2004	02-02-2004
Road 3	Village	56456312	name1	1154	4452	6	03-03-2001	06-05-2005

The lag information for internal use during this project was built on the same data, where we analyzed whether the average loss for this group had declined and if it occurred in fewer cases. The lag information in relation to the overall project was whether there was an overall churn-reducing effect, which did occur since the telecom company had become a less attractive target for this sort of criminal activity.

RESULTS OF THE PROJECT AND THE NEXT STEPS

The project took off in September 2004. During January 2005, the churn rate came down to the magic 2%. As mentioned, 2004 was a year with a deficit of $1 million. Figures for 2005 showed the value of the project as the company realized a profit of $55 million. The results were published in July 2005 in the national press.

The forward CRM strategy went from a focus on closing the gaps in the bucket to increasing the strengths of its sides or from minimizing churn drivers to maximizing loyalty drivers; one of the differences is that you stop rewarding disloyal customers and start rewarding loyal ones. This happened via customer loyalty programs given to customers who had a minimum spend (silver and gold customers, see Chapter 2) and who earned the right to a number of advantages. Marketing automation concepts were introduced (see the maturity models in Chapter 8) in the form of automated communication with current customers, so that campaigns no longer were executed on a monthly basis, but when the customer behavior indicated that communication should occur. This meant that customers who logged on to the Internet portal never saw the same content because the Web site was optimized based on customer history and their profiles. The lead information was still obtained via data-mining models. The results were similar to the displayed decision tree; depending on their age, subscription, and consumption habits, customers would be offered various phones and telecom products that would fit their individual profiles best.

I am not sure what happened to Ibrahim.

About the Author

Gert H.N. Laursen is head of customer intelligence at Maersk Line, the largest containerized shipping company in the world. He focuses on helping product-oriented organizations become more customer-centered through the use of various data sources, including data warehousing, questionnaires, and one-to-one interviews with customers, first-line staff, sales organizations, and other subject matter experts.

Prior to joining Maersk, he worked as a scientist within psychometrics (how to measure and predict human behavior). He has also worked as an analyst in the Telecommunications industry and as a business intelligence consultant. Laursen received his master's degree in business administration from the Aarhus Business School in Denmark and an executive MBA from Henley Management College. Laursen has been a speaker on business intelligence topics at various conferences like the Global CFO Forum (N.Y.), National Spanish Business Improvement Forum (Madrid), SPSS Forum (Paris), Danish National IT foundation, Oracle, and Miracle (Denmark). To see more, go to www.CA-support.com.

Index